Time Management This Is How I Work 300 Percent Faster

Gaurav Sanjiv Kalangan

Published by Gaurav Sanjiv Kalangan, 2023.

Also by Gaurav Sanjiv Kalangan

Learn Options Strategies Options Basics & Greeks For Stock
Trading By Technical Analysis
Bitcoin, Altcoins & ICOs Learn the Basics of Digital Coins
from Zero
Time Management This Is How I Work 300 Percent Faster

Table of Contents

Copyright

Published by Gaurav Sanjiv Kalangan

Copyright © 2023 Gaurav Sanjiv Kalangan

All rights reserved.

Thank you for having an authorized edition of this book and for complying with copyright law. No part of this book may be reproduced, stored in a retrieval system, or transmitted by any means, electronic, mechanical, photocopying, recording, or otherwise, without written permission from the copyright holder.

Distributed by Gaurav Sanjiv Kalangan

Time Management This Is How I Work 300 Percent Faster

Design and composition by Gaurav Sanjiv Kalangan Cover design by Gaurav Sanjiv Kalangan For permission credits.

To offset the number of trees consumed in the printing of our books, Gaurav Sanjiv Kalangan donates a portion of the proceeds from each printing to the Arbor Day Foundation. Gaurav Sanjiv Kalangan has replaced over 50 trees since 2022.

First Edition

I dedicate this to the dreamers, healers, and givers who deliver value through art and invention, expression, and creation. With all my love.

About

Are you ready to take your productivity to the next level and achieve more in your professional life? Our "300% Productivity: How to Triple Your Job Performance" Book is designed for individuals who want to learn practical strategies and techniques to improve time management, increase focus, and enhance overall work performance.

By mastering the strategies and techniques taught in this Book, you'll significantly improve your productivity, work more efficiently, and achieve greater success in your personal and professional lives. These sought-after skills can open doors to new job opportunities, promotions, and increased personal fulfillment. Don't miss this chance to transform your career and achieve more with our "300% Productivity: How to Triple Your Job Performance" Book.

Take charge of your professional growth and elevate your productivity today. Start experiencing the benefits of increased efficiency and job performance right away!

Introduction

Welcome to the Success Bureau's Book on Time Mastery. By managing time, effectively, you will experience less stress and a better sense of stability in your daily life. Thinking through the details of your day from the places you work to the routines you implement will provide a secure structure.

This enables you to let go of thinking about unnecessary details in order to focus on what is truly important to you.

Optimizing Productivity

Optimizing productivity with time and space, using effective time management techniques provides stability and consistency to daily life. As a result, you'll spend less time worrying about the future and more time focusing on the task at hand. The first thing to consider in mapping out your day is your peak productivity time.

Next, think about where you're most productive. As you visualize your whole day, you are more able to focus on the small pieces. Schedule your time to shine in order to effectively manage your hour by hour and day by day routine. You must first ask yourself what is the time of day that I most thrive? Think for a moment about how your most ideal productive day would go.

Do you take the morning slow? When you get right into work, are you most productive at night? Once you can pinpoint your most productive hours, you'll be better able to work out the rest of your day so you can make the most of your valuable time. Perhaps you found that it's difficult to get productive at all during the day. This frustrating dilemma is one that you can overcome, though it may be a struggle to get going once you're in the flow of your work.

All will come easily. Times of optimal productivity. A 2017 California based research study found that the most productive time of day is around 11 a.m. People are most mentally alert between nine a.m. and 11:00 a.m., you can use this information while scheduling meetings as this is the time where people will be the most attentive. Information has even been found about the months where people are most productive.

The most productive month of the year is typically October. As you walk through the typical layout of your day, picture the parts you might want to change, perhaps there are daily time management habits that you would like to get rid of.

Maybe you have multiple times throughout the day where you find yourself in a productive state. If you can picture your productivity in 90 minute increments, it might make it easier to place those throughout your day or all in one block. What if I only have a limited amount of time? Because life is life, there will always be distractions or needs that are unplanned. If you plan to have four hours to work but you wind up only having one hour, that does not mean the day or the time to be productive has to be completely lost. It can be easy to have an all or nothing mindset when it comes to following a schedule.

If you cannot do all of it, do some of it. Once the schedule has been thrown off, it can seem like the rest of the day will be negatively affected as well. This doesn't need to be the case in order to make the most of your time, all the time. Take the power you have and do everything you can with it. You don't need to rush to your highest priority task. First, assign yourself an hour of work on what will move the needle the most. Whatever will move your head the furthest. Try these tips to make the most out of a limited amount of time. Take it one minute at a time, an hour may not seem like a long time.

However, a lot can happen in ten minutes. It can be easy to let an entire hour fly by without having done anything to minimize distractions. Turn your phone on silent and focus on exactly what is in front of you. Focus on tasks that will move you the most towards your goal in the time you have. Prioritize the tasks that need the most immediate attention, the places that inspire you. When considering the time of day that you are most productive, you must also consider where you are when you're most productive.

Now, envision the setting of your ideal most productive workplace. Look around, are there others around you? What does it sound like? Is it a casual or formal setting? Perhaps you have a favorite coffee shop where you go to work, make a regular habit of going into that place at your most productive time of day. If you're not able to get to your ideal setting, create an atmosphere with other qualities that reflects an ideal work setting. Consider these ideas for places to work, go to a coffee shop, your favorite coffee shop can provide a comfortable and productive familiarity.

A coffee shop is a great place to go to get out of isolation and be around people without being directly interrupted. Join a coworking space. Many cities have coworking spaces, a coworking space has all the amenities of a typical workplace, you can enjoy some great motivation by surrounding yourself with others who are productive. If you already work in an office setting, look around the office to see if you can work in your favorite spot or set up your desk to reflect your work needs. If you need minimal distractions, take or distract items off your desk. Outside, refresh yourself and your mind with nature.

Find a table in the shade and take in nature while diving into a productive state at your house. If you have a workspace where you live, you can add or remove setting elements according to your ideal environment. Be sure to keep your workspace away from where you sleep. Save your bedroom just for sleeping. Who will you work with? Humans are social animals. Some are more social than others. If you find that other people give you energy, consider that fact in choosing where you work. Perhaps you're a social person, but not productive while being social.

Be honest with yourself and make a decision based on how you use your time best. If you have one person or a group of people that you work well around, invite them for a weekly work session and use that time to inspire yourself. Establishing your best work time and setting will propel you to more effective time management. Asking the simple questions of when and where will enable you to create the structure that will handle the rest of your day. Having this environment in place will anchor you to your schedule when obstacles and distractions arise.

Focused Task Management

Focused task management, while working on three things at a time, it can feel like you're getting a lot done. Sometimes a mindset can occur that tells you the more you are doing at once, the more you're getting done. This thinking is false. In fact, the opposite is true. When you focus on just one thing at a time, you will achieve higher quality results, having one thing that you're working on will free up more time.

Moving from one thing to another or focusing on many things at once are two ineffective ways to manage time. You may find yourself beginning a long To-Do list, jumping from task to task at the end of an hour, you may find that you have attempted many tasks, but accomplished none. There are three obstacles that may come up during your day. All of them can adversely affect time management in different ways. These obstacles are multitasking, tasks switching and context switching. Multitasking. Multitasking involves doing many tasks at once that are all related to the same end result. Many people attempt multitasking in an effort to be efficient. In fact, it is often celebrated. However, multitasking is not as effective as some believe.

If you think you're an expert multitasker, think again, for example, you may have experience walking while trying to type an email on your phone. While these are both tasks that you know well, they become much more difficult when they're done at the same time. This is because your attention is split between two tasks instead of one. Task switching, task switching is similar to multitasking and that it involves doing many things at once. However, task switching is even less productive than multitasking.

Task switching occurs while focusing on many things at once that are not related to one specific goal. For example, you may have a conversation on the phone about an upcoming event while writing an outline for a new project. These tasks have nothing to do with each other. You're more likely to miss important details when you're trying to give your attention to two different things at once. It can always be difficult to focus, task switching makes it even harder.

The focused feeling of losing track of time and being in the zone is invigorating and productive. These habits prohibit the ability to get totally lost in your work. Switching from task to task simultaneously means that none of the work produced will be as high in quality as work that is done while only focusing on one thing. There are two types of tasks which an interrupted task, Ritchin and Rapide tasks which an. Interrupted tasks which occur most of the time when you have email, social media and text message notifications.

If you have noise alerts or pop ups on your computer, you're likely to be easily distracted and pulled out of the moment you're having with your work. If you're in a flow state, totally focused and even enjoying yourself, that can all be lost with a simple notification. An example of this unfortunate interruption is illustrated by our biggest distraction, social media. Once you notice a new social media notification, the moment you click on it, you have officially switched. You may be working on the project in one window while checking social media on the next.

These interruptions are a major obstacle in time management, they inhibit you from entering the flow states required to get done what you need to. Rapid task switching. Rapid tasks which involve switching from task to task in rapid succession. Taking notes on your notebook with your computer open to another task is one surefire way to fall into rapid task switching. You may move from typing an email to writing an outline for a project you're working on in the same second. Going from task to task in quick succession diminishes awareness, not just of your work, but of the rest of the world around you as well. It limits your ability to think clearly and with care.

Context switching. Context switching occurs when you go from one task to an entirely different task, this is different from multitasking and task switching and that it does not involve doing many tasks at once. Context switching means moving from one project to another without completing either project. If you have eight hours in your work time, choose your most important project and work on that in order to use your time most effectively to complete that first project before moving on to anything else. If you move from Project A before it's done, you're likely to end up with two unfinished projects by the end of the day instead of one whole task done.

A huge disadvantage to context, which is that it wastes precious work time once you've come out of focus. It takes about 25 minutes to get into another state of focus. If you switch context three times in your day, you've lost over an hour of time that could have been expertly well spent. Strategies have no fear. Though there are many things that come up that are so much to get done with so little time, it's possible to prevent these distracting habits, use these strategies to focus on just one thing at a time. One, implement the when and where of your work environment. When you're in your ideal work setting, you're more likely to become engulfed in your work to make it a rule to complete a task before you begin the next one. This will increase your work endurance and will help you get more done.

You won't waste such precious time. Three Turn off all your social media and email notifications. Turn all of your technology onto Do Not Disturb mode. You can even have an auto message letting people know when you'll be back online or stay away from distracting websites. You may have a habit of typing in your favorite websites when you're really meant to check your email. You can avoid this by using applications and reminders that will protect you from distracting websites. Five. Take advantage of sound, put on your favorite background noise, or eliminate background noise altogether with noise canceling headphones.

Prioritizing Daily Tasks

Prioritizing daily tasks, mastering time management doesn't come easily. It takes practice and consistency. The best way to ensure that you get everything done on your list is by prioritizing the most important tasks and doing them first. Prioritization skills come with practice and may not always be clear what exactly is most important, though some projects have steps. Others are more general and could be accomplished in a variety of ways. Pick out the tasks that are most sure to move forward.

Ask yourself if I complete this task, will I be satisfied with what I have done? Consider the item that you would do if you could only choose one thing to do. Which task would move you closer to your goal in the allotted time? It can be difficult to know where to start when it comes to prioritizing a to do list full of important tasks. You can begin the process by talking with others about how they prioritize their work. You can also look at your old habits. Consider whether your current work habits are sustainable. Do you find yourself with many incomplete tasks during the week?

Do you miss deadlines? These might be signs that you need to look at the big picture and re prioritize your items. Follow this proven process to prioritize your tasks. One starts by making a list of everything you need to do, you can make a list that covers the entire week and then break it down in day by day sections to write any deadlines or time constraints while observing your list. This will help you determine when you need to start working on what. Be sure to consider the size of each project and deadline three the night before each workday. Look at your list and visualize your day.

What are the tasks that you can get done in your designated work? Time for set aside tasks that are unnecessary or not pertinent to what you're currently trying to get done. Look at how you want to spend the day and set aside tasks that don't relate to the objectives you have for your day five. It's helpful to start on the most dreadful or difficult task. First, if you first accomplish something that you don't want to do, you'll feel less burdened and more motivated.

Six You can use all of these things to set your priorities straight, take a step back and weigh the importance of each task according to the goals you have in mind. Remain flexible that are bound to be distractions. New things pop up, surprises occur, and important phone calls come in. Even though you planned out your day the night before, there are days where nothing goes as planned or things get pushed back. When these unexpected turns occur, you can use your priorities to guide you towards the task to focus on when you do have time. If you have an impending deadline or particularly difficult task, begin with those, if you're asked to take on too many practice boundaries and avoid promising more than you can deliver.

Use your time wisely, carefully. Consider your high priority items as you look at each day. Take advantage of your most productive hours by doing the items that need your utmost attention. Use your time wisely by knowing how things are going to go and give care to each minute.

Pay Attention to Your Time

Pay attention to your time. There are 1440 minutes, and each day most people are awake for about 16 hours out of the day. That means you have about nine hundred and sixty minutes to do what you need to do in order to have a successful day. This may seem daunting or it may seem inspiring. Regardless, it's important to be cognizant of the way you spend your time. On average, humans are able to focus for about 20 minutes at a time, however, it's possible to be focused for 20 minutes and then repeatedly refocus.

You can use this information to your advantage when you estimate how long each task will take. If something will take four hours, look at it in 20 minute sections. How much of this project can you get done in 20 minutes? How much can you get done in one hour? Take planned breaks. Maintain your attention on each task, but make sure to take a break every 90 minutes if 90 minutes seems too long. You can also take breaks every 15 minutes, 15 to 20 minutes is a perfect length of time to give your brain a refreshing break. You can practice being mindful of your time by being mindful during your timed breaks, practicing a quick mindfulness activity is more effective than taking a break to get on social media or read the news.

Mindfulness enables you to calm your mind and come to the present moment. Social media stimulates the mind and distracts from the present moment. Try these mindfulness activities during work breaks, one, meditate, you can meditate for just a few minutes, sit up straight in your chair, close your eyes or focus on one point ahead of you. Start to simply pay attention to your breath. Notice I am inhaling. I am excited to go on a walk. Embrace the feeling of fresh air and sunshine by taking it a step away from your work and going on a walk.

Leave your phone behind, simply observe and notice the greenery, the sound of the cars and the color of the sky. Three, take a coloring break, grab a coloring book and set a timer for 10 minutes. Use those minutes to relax and color. This exercise will help keep your mind engaged without thinking about other things. For your five senses, take a moment to notice all of your senses. What do you hear, see, smell, taste and feel? Go through all of your muscle groups and relax them, starting with your toes and ending with your ears, set reminders for yourself to help notify you of an upcoming transition in your day. These small alerts can serve as a line of accountability when you're trying to practice new habits. If you notice a thing five minutes before it's time to move on to your next task, you'll be able to find a stopping point and make a smooth transition to the next item of business.

You can also take advantage of the opportunity that Mellat presents. Use a small moment in your transition to acknowledge your day and check that your focus is on the task at hand. You don't always have to stop what you're doing in order to be mindful. You can take advantage of moments at work where you can bring your attention to exactly what you are doing. If your next task calls for movement, bring your focus to your walking, feel the ground beneath your shoes and focus on your breath, even if it's just for a moment.

It's easy to look to the future and concern ourselves with imagined scenarios that we truly cannot predict. These small moments of mindfulness can provide a chance to let go of worry and focus on the task at hand without disrupting your day. How does mindfulness affect productivity? An ability to focus on the present moment brings about a stronger connection to the task at hand rather than your entire To-Do list. Those who practice mindfulness have been shown to be less affected by distractions. Mindfulness increases productivity by creating a manageable stream of thoughts that do not overwhelm.

By practicing mindfulness regularly, you're likely to increase your ability to regulate emotions. This stability provides focus on only the thoughts that count. Treat your time with care and attention, the best way to be mindful of your time is to be aware and conscious of what you do. And when you do it, you can do this by creating a system, a routine for each day.

Setting Up Your Daily System

Setting up your daily system, time management isn't just about getting stuff done. Time management is about structure and consistency. Structure provides a sense of security and relief to each day it decreases the need for worry or time wasting thoughts. If you already know how the first three hours of your day are going to go, you don't need to wake up and wonder how the next three hours will go. You already know because you have a system. Follow a routine.

Working within a structure, no matter how subtle, provides numerous benefits by having a routine, you're more likely to not just be more productive, but also to feel better all around. You'll get sound asleep, feel less stressed and have a stronger ability to focus on each task at each designated time of day. You can begin thinking about your routine by splitting your day into sections, beginning with the first hour.

What does the first hour of your day look like? Try to spend the first hour of your day away from technology. Avoid checking your email or responding to text messages, take the first hour of your day just for yourself so you can transition into your daily life. By preparing, thinking through and strategizing for the day ahead, you'll feel a greater sense of stability. Ask yourself these questions about your routine one morning.

- What is the first thing you want to do each morning?

- What is the second thing you want to do each morning?

- What will make your morning feel like a success?

- What is the most important daily task you'll do each morning?

- Two nightly routines, how do you want to end your day?

- How will you wind down from your day?

- What is the most important task you want to do each night?

- What task would help you feel a sense of completion about your day?

- What are the most important things you want to get done in the morning, accumulate small successes early on in your day?

This will help you feel confident and ready for your day. For example, you can start your day by making your bed, though this may seem insignificant. Maybe your bed starts shortly in a refreshingly successful way. It lets you know that you are officially beginning your day. It gives you success right away. And a nicely made bed is waiting for you at the end of each day. Think about the rest of your day in sections as well.

What do you do before you work? When do you take breaks, when do you eat, consider these questions as you walk yourself through your day. Once you have basic routines that take care of the little stuff, take a look at your long term goals to come up with a daily system, create your system based on what's right in front of you. Though you have goals, having a system is actually a better use of your time and productivity, what Is the difference between goals and systems? Goals are important. They motivate us to become the people we are meant to be.

They guide us through the storms of life by providing a light at the end of the tunnel that determines our values and the way we live our lives. We look at the future and the bigger picture of our life in the long term when we set goals, systems are also important systems zoom in on the day to day and minute to minute details on the actions that will bring your long term goals to fruition. However, if you spend all your time looking at the goal on the horizon, you might lose track of what is right in front of you instead of only focusing on the future. Look at this exact moment.

Look at each moment and the role it plays in propelling you to success. In order to create your system and the most effective way, you must start by setting your goals. Big picture goals are based on the lifestyle and career paths that you want to pursue. Systems are the building blocks to those goals. Follow this process to set long term goals, one, consider your values, what do you consider success? Do you want to accumulate a fortune accolade? Think about what your life will look like when you feel that you've reached your full potential to zoom in on one aspect of your desired outcome. For example, consider what job you would like to have.

What kind of person do you want to be five years from now? What would you like to have accomplished? Three times your goals realistically think about how long it might take you to get to your goal. This will help you visualize your goal. Be careful not to take on too much. You want to set yourself up for success instead of disappointment. Building a system, once you have a long term goal set in place, you'll be able to set up your day to day system, break down your goal into six month intervals next. Break it into one month intervals. Finally, think about the specific things you need to do on a daily or weekly basis to take constant steps towards the official destination.

Your system consists of your daily things you do and focus on that move you forward towards your long term goal. By creating your daily system, you'll be able to let go of the future and focus on enjoying the present moment. You won't need to worry about your goal when you're following your system, because success is built into each day. For example, imagine you have a goal to write a 300 page book in one year. What do you need to do each day to reach that goal? By breaking down each page into month sections and taking one day off per week, you could realistically write 500 words per day. So at what time of day would you write to build your system based on your long term goal?

When there's a long term goal, the small step supports that goal. You don't need to keep your eyes on the prize. You only need to keep your eyes on this present moment. By doing this, you will experience less stress and a greater likelihood of success. The steps you take each day to work towards the finish line can be seamlessly placed through each part of your day, setting up the rest of your day to reflect the goals you want to work towards.

Set a Schedule

Set a schedule, stick to it, lay out your entire day by creating a realistic schedule of your day to day system in order to make the most effective use of your time and be the most productive, map out the hours and hours details that comprise each of your day's. Before you schedule anything, take a look at the way you're currently spending your time. Take one week to observe each hour of your day.

Documents the way you currently spend your time. This exercise will help you create a structure that can provide support and help you make the most use of your time with the least amount of stress. An example of a schedule on a typical day, seven a.m. to eight a.m., wake up, make bed, meditate, eat breakfast, 8am to 9:00 a.m., go to work, review To-Do list and priorities. Check email, 9:00 a.m. to 12:00 p.m. Work on tasks in order of priority. Take planned breaks at least every 90 minutes.

Reduce the scope, you don't need to do everything all in one day if you put too much on your plate, you wind up losing more time and producing less work. Imagine a doctor who puts too many patients in one day. If there's any disturbance in the schedule, the waiting room will grow more crowded as the wait gets longer, reducing the scope of your day and focusing only on what is realistic if you end up taking on too much. It will be harder to follow a schedule.

A full plate is a catalyst for stress and incomplete work. Be quick, but don't hurry. Avoid overwhelming yourself in order to be efficient. Leave no task untouched. Maintain the order of your day to the best of your ability. If you have a daily routine you want to follow, stick to it. Follow the order of each event, even if you no longer have the planned amount of time. For example, if you plan to clean your house for an hour but only have 20 minutes, you can focus on one room and get that done.

This habit will also help you maintain your daily schedule in the long run, even if it doesn't work on one day. Things may not be going as planned, but time can still be used wisely, even though not everything was accomplished. The feeling of success will still come after doing everything that you could. Batching, when you pack your days, you complete tasks that are similar to each other in sections, for example, you might have one hour on your schedule to check emails and return phone calls.

You can split your day's intersections and create a streamlined organization. There seems to be a culture that encourages constant email check in, however, new research suggests checking email just three times per day. For some, this sounds stressful. The fear of missing out comes into play, which makes checking email irresistible. This habit is a difficult one to break. You can start small. Check your email five times per day.

You can even let people know that all of their emails will be responded to within 24 hours. Social media is a huge part of the daily life of many people. It has become a natural way to communicate and connect with those within our community and throughout the world. Social media can also be as addictive as checking email. A healthy habit to implement is one of conscious social media time, rather than check in notifications, every time there is a free moment, choose a time of day that you're dedicated to social media patching categories.

Here are some examples of categories that may work well for your time management when you patch them together. One Professional correspondents check email, return phone calls to social hour, check text messages, coordinate social plans, check social media, three current events, check in on the news, get updates on topics of interest for self-improvement. Go to the gym. Work towards your long term goal. You can examine the rest of your schedule and look at your most productive time of day in order to choose where you batch which tasks use your productivity, time to your advantage and create a schedule according to which tasks need the most attention.

There are even days of the week where you might want to take care of an entire category of tasks. Three more days, some activities don't need to be done every day, for example, you might not need to go to the grocery store every day. Activities that can be put on just one day can be categorized into themes for your days. If you have multiple errands to do each week, choose just one day to do all of them. These themes are part of your weekly rituals and habits that you want to maintain over time. Whether you take your dog to the dog park once a week or choose one day each week to have meetings with co-workers doing them on the same day, each week will create a stable consistency.

Consider the suggested themes, mastery, Monday's practice, a new hobby, improve on a new skill, productivity Tuesdays, complete big projects, schedule meetings for this day, dedicate extra focus to work, work out Wednesdays, schedule a longer workout session, work with a personal trainer. Thinking of your weeks in sections like this helps you to focus on the day ahead rather than the months or years ahead. Make time for fun, create time to pursue the things you love that are not work related. A great way to reward yourself after satisfying a hard day of work is by engaging in one of your hobbies. Productivity is essential. Embracing hobbies is also an essential way to avoid burnout.

When you schedule your day and prioritize your tasks, you'll be better able to make time for the things you love. If you find that you have so much on your plate that you don't have time for fun, the solution isn't to eliminate fun. Instead, start by carving out as little as an hour per week to dedicate to a hobby whether you most enjoy cross stitching, rock climbing or juggling. You can make time for both your high priority responsibilities and your extracurricular hobbies. It can be difficult to find hobbies as life takes over. Time flies by as the hustle and bustle determines how our days go.

By taking charge and making positive changes in your time management skills, you'll suddenly find that you have more free time to dedicate to fostering a well-rounded lifestyle short on fun. Use these techniques to choose a new hobby. One. Make a list. Write down all the things you're interested in. You don't need to have an end plan in mind. Just jot down the first things that come to mind.

For example, you may be interested in astrology, painting and filmmaking too. Once you have a list of interests, choose a couple to try out by exploring a new hobby. You'll broaden your horizons and have a stronger ability to approach work with a fresh outlook. Three Avoid limiting yourself. You don't have to have just one hobby. You can pursue a number of things you're interested in.

The Bottom Line

The bottom line, take inventory of your daily life and let go of the habits that no longer serve you, acquiring new time management skills will foster a greater spark or productivity that will endure through the obstacles that naturally arise. You don't have to expend energy and worry about the organization of your day.

Regular practice and implementation of a few simple skills can actually save you time so that you can better focus on what is pertinent to the current moment. Follow this process to integrate effective time management skills into your daily routine. Step one, begin by considering when you're most productive, take stock of what your days currently look like and make realistic adjustments in order to use your time more effectively.

Use your highest alert times to take care of your highest priority items, schedule your meetings and free time according to the ebb and flow of your day. Create your ideal setting for productivity. Think about where you feel the most comfortable. Find an accessible and consistent setting where you can focus and get into the flow of your workday step to choose one task to focus on at a time. Let go of old multitasking habits that hold productivity, diminish work quality, and stir up more stress use strategies that will limit distractions. This will help you maintain focus.

It takes around 25 minutes to refocus on a task once you've broken focus, switching from task to task is unproductive and will end up wasting time. It's best to focus on each task as it comes to completing one task before moving on to the next. A day with one complete project is more successful than a day with two incomplete projects. Step three, examine the importance of each task ahead of you, depending upon time constraints and level of focus. Prioritize your tasks.

Begin your work time with the most important task. Despite all of the planning in the world, many days go in a different direction than intended, remaining flexible in the face of distraction or interruption. Referring to your priorities list can help you make decisions about how you use a limited amount of time. Step four. Be attentive of your time. Take care to notice how you spend each day. The day does not need to be daunting or overwhelming. Planned mindfulness breaks will help the day go by at an even pace.

Take a step back after around 90 minutes of work time, in doing so, you'll be able to maintain a consistent work pace and quality of focus. Follow a simple and consistent routine. Think of your day in sections, consider what each part of your day looks like, beginning with the moment you wake up, step five, develop and sustain an efficient system in which you will thrive. A system is created based on your long term goals. Instead of constantly looking towards the future, bring your attention to what you can do each day that will inevitably lead to your goals.

Goals are based on the long term big picture ideas for your life. Systems are the small daily steps that lead to achievement of those long term goals, step six creates a schedule that works for you. Be careful not to take on more than you can handle. Knowing your limits is good for you, good for your work, and good for the people around you. If your daily schedule is disturbed, do your best to get to every task. If you planned an hour, but only have 20 minutes, spend a focused, productive 20 minute period on the scheduled task.

Categorize sections of your days based on the similarity of different tasks, if you have administrative tasks to do, do them all in the same part of your day, spend less time checking your email schedule times to check your email and take care of those responses during planned parts of your day. Pursuing hobbies. Making time for intentional fun ensures a consistent and stress free quality of life. Though life may sometimes seem too busy for hobbies, you can make time for them when you implement effective time management skills, a natural consequence of time management is an increase in productivity.

Distractions and worries are minimized when your days are predictable and simple. Consistent and regular practice of these time management tools are the catalyst for innovation and growth.

Thank you

That brings us to the end of this Book, congratulations for completing all of the chapters on behalf of everyone here at the Success Bureau. I would like to wish you the very best for the future and hope to see you again soon.

Working from Home Effectively

Working From Home is becoming increasingly popular, available and empowering! Imagine if you could work for any company in the world and not just those that are based in your city or country. Or imagine if you had more flexibility to care for your family, renovate your home, or start a business. Working From Home is a commonly misunderstood and understudied skill, but if done right it can truly transform your career and open a lot of new doors. Despite increasingly becoming a part of our everyday lives, amazingly, most people are never taught how to be effective in making your own schedule and workspace. So, in this Book, you'll be walked through step by step on how to simply and effectively manage your time and space at home, regardless of your industry and personality type.

This Book covers everything you need to know about running a Home Business, working in Virtual Teams, or even Working Abroad. Essentially any situation where you might need to spend a day at home instead of in an office building, but still be productive, focused, organized and Of course happy. We focus on extremely practical actionable changes you can make to ensure Working From Home is just as effective as working in an office... Perhaps even more! You'll learn whether a daily routine is truly essential, tech and tools to make life easier, mastering virtual calls (as a guest or a host) and creating a brilliant office space at home. Say goodbye to feeling low energy, distracted and unmotivated, and instead enjoy the simplicity of building your own schedule. This Book covers detailed tips for excellent planning using Gantt Charts and PERT diagrams, managing a team, avoiding overspend, predicting risks and dealing with multiple stakeholders.

After this Book, you will feel calm, collected, well prepared and confident that you can work effectively from anywhere. You'll know how to create your own schedule and find your own motivation and goals. We look at lots of real-life software and set up examples and give you practical tools you can use right away to get better results in your day. Whether you're a solopreneur with a home business, or part of global virtual teams this Book will empower you as someone who is always one step ahead.

By becoming productive and effective at Working From Home, not only will you pave the way for a future promotion, but you'll also have transformed your own personal happiness and freedom potential!

Who this Book is for

1. Those already working from home, or aspiring to
2. People in virtual teams or remote companies
3. Someone who wants to run a Home Business as an entrepreneur, self employed or freelancer
4. A person who works either full time or part time away from their main office
5. Anyone who would love to be able to travel or work abroad via remote work
6. Someone who would enjoy increased freedom, flexibility and autonomy to make their own schedule and work environment choices.

Introduction

Welcome to this Book now. This cause is split into three chapters, the first chapter is all to do with self care, and it's aimed in particular at the growing number of people who are working from home. I go through a series of self care exercises or activities that you can do whilst working at home.

I'm assuming that if you're working at home, you can still take a few minutes here or there. For example, if you are dealing with Zoome conferences or you're working with other people or you're working online, there's nothing to stop you, for example. I'm just drawing whilst you're talking. So, for example, you could draw your boss or for example, you could even try drawing without even looking down at all, perhaps to express your frustration at all things that are piling up on you.

And so you just make a drawing. And I'm not saying that you should do this in the middle of a conversation with other people, but you could do it while still perhaps reading someone's email. And if you're reading people's email, then all the time you've got to think about you've got to think about priorities. How much can you control within your circle of influence? What gives you hope, hope about your work perhaps, or about your home life? And that's supposed to be time and balance. So there's me in the middle and considerations around.

Now I just do that real time. That's what I did before real time while I was talking to the camera. So the point about these exercises is you can do some of them, perhaps by looking at emails and you can do some of them when you have a short break, because surely you don't get up at eight thirty and then work for nine hours, taking the break between one and two. Yes, you need a routine, but it needs a routine.

If you're working from home that is set by you, you are saving time in commuting, for example. That can also be a disadvantage because at the end of the day, you may find out you've only walked. Twenty steps or something, and all you've done is walk from or get up from your bed to the desk to the bathroom to the kitchen, to the bathroom, to the desk, back to bed. And that's all you've done all day. Yeah. You may have a booklet or some chapters about doing bodyweight exercises or press ups or something, or you may even have a few weights.

But if you're working from your bedroom, even if it's a big bedroom, perhaps you live in a shared house and normally you do this outside, but now you've got to in your bedroom. So the point is these self care exercises are what you can do at work, at home. Now, the second chapter consists of a series of visualizations. And these you can do at the end of the day, beginning today, probably at the end of the day, is better. Now, this applies when you get home from work, if you're going out to work or when you've finished your work, work at home. So a series of visualizations.

The third chapter is a whole series of office games. Now you can play at work, assuming you go to an office of his games. However, be warned and there are warnings with each of these games, playing these games can be dangerous. You could lose your job with some of them, like clambering over desks, for example. So I've also included a whole load of tips that go down the side. If you owe my side, I should say, to go down the side of me about improving your well-being. So that's the format. Self care, home visualizations, office games. OK, let's get started.

Meditative Art - part 1

Welcome to this chapter. This is all about meditating, but through art, so the first thing is that you do not not make a plan. You are going to be drawing, yes, but you don't sit and think, oh, I'm going to be drawing a lighthouse or a house with many windows or a house with different paths or a fork in the path, and which choice do I take it or do I end up in the middle? No, no, no. I mean, you might end up doing that, but you're not going to plan your drawing.

So what you are going to do if you're following this exercise, which obviously I hope you do, is that you allow the colors, the range of colors to have different patterns or felt tip pens or board markers or crayons or. Any different colors in front of you and you allowed them to choose you? Which color do you feel most drawn towards? But today I'm here to talk about color, psychology, the study of hues as detriments to human behavior.

Now, I know color psychology already sounds mildly fishy. I mean, how could something as simple as just color really affect us that much? Well. The color orange affects the color orange makes you more hungry, whereas the color blue is an appetite suppressant. The color pink has been found to calm violent prisoners, whereas extreme amounts of the color yellow make the babies cry. And that's only a few ways that colors can affect us. So I decided to conduct my own little experiment.

I drew three different pictures and then made duplicates of each picture where the only thing that changed were the colors in the pictures. The first one I changed the colors that printed the entire drawing. The second one I changed the entire monochrome palette. And then the third one, I only changed one of the two colors. I would show each pair of pictures to people and then ask them a question that corresponded with each one.

Now, you may have read or visited websites where they talk about how different colors mean different things to people. If you haven't, it doesn't matter. This is not about educating you about colors and why you chose a particular color. This Book, this chapter is about doing, doing, doing, doing so. Let's say, for example, that you've reached out. Well, I didn't know which color. Now, I think I choose green, which is a peaceful color, by the way, and I think I'll choose green. What are you going to draw? Who knows?

You don't know because you're not going to plan it. You just follow whatever impulses come up. Doesn't matter if they are silly. Doesn't matter if you can't draw, it doesn't matter if what you draw is a hideous drawing or something quite well drawn. It's something horrific. That's not the point. You just follow whatever impulses come up. No, we are not. And this is all about the process. And that's the point about art therapy. We are not judging what you draw. It is simply the process. And if you don't like what you draw, then you can just cut up. I drew this in an earlier chapter. Maybe I like it. Maybe I don't. Maybe I want to change things. Maybe I want to change to have for example, maybe I want to put the drawing on some sort of block perhaps, which is all pretty hideous, maybe some sort of trophy.

For example, I saw one recently with golden hair and no mustache and it was a cartoon. I think it might have been something to do with the presidential election anyway. Now, if you don't like what you saw or you didn't like the process, I've just voted out for neatness. But you could just screw it up. You could tear it up, just tear it up and just throw it away. And in so doing, you have let go of your attachment because you throw it away and we assume it's no longer in your mind. So you've thrown it away, it's left your mind as well.

You've let go of your attachment to the product. Because. The actual product imposed on the process, the process was making it get rid of the product and we were only interested in the process. Now, you've drawn whatever you've drawn with whatever color you've felt drawn to.

Meditative Art - part 2

Now you've got to pay attention to your senses, see what your senses are noticing whilst you are drawing with your panel, you know, crying or your biro, your fountain pen or your board marker, whatever whilst you were drawing, how the implement you were using. What did it feel like? In your hand, as you were drawing, this is just a pen against a table as you were drawing, was it making any sound, perhaps squeaking if it was a bold marker?

Was it making any sound as you moved back and forth? What are you pressing harder in some areas than others, softer in some areas? And if you are using different art materials, let's say you were painting. What did the art materials smell like? So we've got sound. We've got a site. We've got how it felt as you were painting or drawing and how it smelled as well. Now, music therapy, whilst you were drawing, maybe there was a sound or sounds in the background. Maybe you are unfortunate enough to live in a noisy area. And so you constantly had traffic and airplanes and children and dogs and everything.

Well, maybe you live in the countryside up to a point. Yes, you could close the window if it's noisy outside, but that's about it. Perhaps choose the quietest room, but you could generate sound, perhaps put on music to make it instrumental. We don't want you to be distracted by the lyrics or perhaps put on something that's in a foreign language, a language that you don't understand, and that you don't find particularly hostile or aggressive or unpleasing or displeasing because we don't want you to focus on the words just on the sound.

Now, maybe whatever you've done is just a series of dots or circles or a series of doodles. It doesn't matter. We're not after any particular design. It's just a process. Open yourself up. Use your senses. Whatever the product is, finish it. Or you can take a picture of it. Post it in the question answer chapter for this chapter, but be aware of the process. Now you're working from home, remember you could set yourself a time limit for this perhaps 60 seconds, perhaps 90, perhaps a minute, and just do the drawing. Make the drawing.

Participate in the process at the end of the minute. Doesn't matter what you've done. What matters is how did you feel doing it and how do you feel now? So I'm going to tell you I don't worry about the time. It's going to be exactly one minute, I'm going to put a picture up on the screen. You don't have to look at it. Your drawing may not be related to it at all. But just do the drawing for one minute. Get your materials while I'm talking.

Grab some materials, get some paper, get some pens or crayons or paint. Get yourself organized because you haven't got them immediately to hand because you're working from home. In fact, maybe you're reading this when really, you should be working. Hmm. Anyway, getting the materials perhaps feels dependent. They're easier to make a squeaky noise, but they're easier to use. I'm going to put something quite nice up on the screen. Thank you.

Block of Nine

Welcome to this chapter. This is very, very straightforward. Several different alternatives. Pack of cards now, this is a company. I invested in crowdfunding many years ago, and they produced these cards. I'm going to just show you one. It's not particularly important. Now, that's just what I put. Activating the G 20 minutes is good, do whatever you can manage. Here's another one. Call someone at random. And these are called practice cards.

Now there are several options here. You could just get a piece of paper and all you could do on screen and make a series of grids, perhaps say three columns by three nine squares cut them up. So in a sense, you're creating your own card. And then on each little box. So if you've got nine, this will last you, let's say, two a day. So you've got four and a half days where you're working from home, you're working five days a week, for example.

And so for the nine into each box, one a day in the morning, one a day. In the afternoon, so Friday afternoon, we're leaving blank for the moment. And you just doodle. Do, too, for about four or five minutes. Just whatever comes to mind or. And you could put, for example, in the box a drawing of an emotion. You are feeling anger, hate, love, peacefulness, kindness, loneliness. Or you could put an affirmation now in terms of affirmations, what you could do is Google affirmations or sayings or something like that. And then it could.

Copy and paste them into a document or similar, print them out, cut them up, put them into a bowl instead of having a bowl of flowers, you could have a bowl of affirmation, so you take one out as your affirmation for the day. You could then put that in the card that's up to you. So you got doodles or emotions or. Affirmations. Well, just blatant. And then on the Friday afternoon, remember you've got nine one in the morning, 1:00 in the afternoon, Monday, Tuesday, Wednesday, Thursday, eight plus Friday morning. You've now got nine cards, so you just take one at random.

Now, if it's negative because of the emotion you are particularly upset at the time. Then you just got it. Throw it away. If it's positive, you're particularly happy, relaxed, the business is going well, you just had a very good Zoom meeting, just had a good report, you just clinched a deal. You'd have double the amount of inquiries. The normal thing, keep that. For the next week and over a period of time, you're going to end up with nine three by three nine positive cards. Remember, you've cut this up and you can keep those, perhaps put them on something like this on which perhaps normally you'd put on a smartphone or something.

And if ever you're fed up at work, just take one of the cards that you created and these if their emotions, then you know how you felt at the time. If there are affirmations, no, they're not yours, but they are the ones you selected. And if they're just doodles. Then you can just take the doodle, maybe interpret it in a different way. These are just examples. But the point about this is you're in effect. You are creating. Your own set of cards based on your work that you have at work, actually, if you're working in an office, you could take it to the office, can you? But this is particularly aimed at people working at home.

I've seen packs of cards that are exercises as well. So you take a card and then you suddenly do 10 press ups or something, you could put something like that as one of the cards, a fitness or health activity. Or a random act of kindness that can be done from the room, like phoning up a friend, but is that just going to take two or three minutes? And is that really something you should be doing while you're working at home? I think not, and this is only to take food one, two, three, four or five minutes, we're talking about very small self-care activities.

So what I'm going to do, I'm just going to put something nice on the screen and some music. I just like you to do just one of these. So Creatinine cards, or maybe just two, if you want to make them pretty big. And just to start you off dirt while these images are in front of you. Posting the question answer chapter. Let me know how it goes. Thank you.

Time to Breathe

So you managed to set a routine. You get up at 6:50, which is what you used to do before, when you had to commute to work, get out your shower all the time, your steel cut oats beginning to cook because you planned it, you soaked them the night before and you put them on a low heat on the stove. But with water, Of course, because you're later going to put on black strap molasses for the potassium with banana as well because you like a healthy breakfast, but you've got your routine. 06:50 Get up in the shower.

Perhaps before the shower you do five minutes worth of bodyweight exercises. Perhaps you do some squats, some lunges, some press ups, some curls. Or maybe you just stretch or maybe grounding. You walk outside in the garden, but it's snowing, always pouring with rain. Now it's so cold in November, almost like a post. Presidential election chill. Anyway, you have your routine. You go and eat your steel cut oats, or perhaps your muesli. Or perhaps your fruit, not high carb bread, not super sweet sugary honey on the toast. No, no, no, no. Perhaps you have your green tea.

Perhaps you have a garlic drink. Anyway, the point is you have your routine. You then turn up to work, i.e. in the room you set to one side for you to work at home, which just might be your bedroom. Or maybe the kitchen downstairs. Keep the kids away. Keep everybody else away because you are working at home and you concentrate and you do all the emails that you need to do, you have completed the spreadsheets, you've scheduled a meeting. You've done several callbacks to people who made inquiries or halfway through the report, and everything's up to date.

But you're beginning to get a bit tired, you have been focused for two or three hours, and if you had a pedometer on, you've actually only walked about 100 steps and that included going to the fridge to get the milk or going to the fridge to get cold water, going to the fridge to get the iced tea that you put in much earlier, perhaps even last night. But you haven't worked very much and you haven't been outside, but you can't stress that what you need is a breathing space, so you can do this at home.

Remember, because you are at home and this is the whole point of these exercises. These are aimed at people who work from home. So this is a five minute breathing space practice. I'm going to now disappear. Can I put some tea party on the screen, photograph, perhaps, or paint something really to help you relax, but you're not really looking at the screen, you're just listening to me. So are you ready? It's going on the screen now. What I would like you to do is if you're sitting down or lying down, become physically still, maybe you have a standing desk and you've been reading this chapter. Standing so whatever you're doing, lying, sitting or standing. Be still physically still.

Also, be as comfortable as possible if you're standing, try and ensure that you have no shoes or socks on standard bare feet. If you're sitting set upright, posture is important. If you're lying down, stretch out and then relax. Likely close your eyes. Bring your awareness to whatever is going on for you right now. Give the weight of your body. Up to gravity. Allow your weight to sink into the points of contact between your body and the floor. The chair. Or bed? What sensations are there right now? If you notice any tension. Or resistance? Towards painful or unpleasant sensations.

Gently turn towards them. Accept them. As best you can. If you begin to tense around the breath. Then let go a little bit more with each breath. Soften into gravity. Notice any thoughts as they arise and pass through the mind. Observe them. See if you can let them come and go. Without beginning to identify with their content. Observe them as if they were clouds in the sky. Notice any feelings and emotions as they arise. Can you let these come and go? Include everything within your awareness with a kindly perspective?

Now, allow your awareness to gather around the experience of the breath deep in the body. Drop your awareness inside the breath and feel the different sensations in the front. The back. And signs of the torso. Can you feel your awareness within the flow and movement? Of the breadth. Use the breath to anchor your awareness in the present moment. Breathing in the body. Noticing each inhale. And exhale again and again and again, breathe in. Pause. And exhale each time you notice your mind has wandered gently, guide the mind back to the breath deep in the body.

Now gently expand your awareness to include the whole body, feel the weight. And the shape of the body as it sits. Stands or lies? If you've got any pain or discomfort? Make sure your awareness stays open. Cultivate acceptance or acknowledgement for all of your experience. Befriend it, use the breath to anchor your awareness in the present moment. Breathing in the body, noticing each inhale. And exhale. Inhale, pause, exhale. Again and again and again. When you're ready. Go back to work.

Set and Intention

Welcome to this chapter. Now this chapter is really well, it's about one word and intention, yes, intention. If you go to yoga classes, you might have heard your yoga instructor say. Set an intention. For your practice, and so you could set an intention for that particular practice or that particular day or that particular week, the month for the year, depending on when you see this.

You could set your intention just for the time period before Christmas or just the Christmas break or just New Year's Day or the whole of the New Year. Of course, you set your own intention. But how can you do it and what might it be? Well, how can you remind yourself of the intention that you said what you could do is set an alarm for your intention? So, for example, on your computer, you set an alarm every hour or every three hours or whatever every morning, and your intention could come up on the screen could be a screensaver or it's simply a buzzer to remind you of the intention that you set and sort of like a little flash on your face just to remind you so you could set an alarm.

You could actually put it on a post-it note. Stick it on your alarm clock. So when you wake up in the morning at 5:00 or 6:00 because you obviously get up at sunrise to meditate or to walk out in the garden grounding things or be out with nature in the pouring rain. And maybe not, but you could put the intention on your alarm clock. Yes, or even pin it onto clients or something. You could write it in your daily planner.

You could put it on your toothpaste, then you'd see it twice or three times a day, or you could put it on the mirror in your bathroom. You could put it on the toilet seat on the inside. No, not inside the bowl, inside the lid. So you take the lid up and there's your intention, abundance or oneness.

What sort of intention for the toilet seat? But still, you could make a background for your computer flashes up every so often. That is your intention. You could do all of this. Obviously, you could write a small paragraph about why you have this intention. And then look at it on a regular basis, particularly if it's on your smartphone. So those are just some ideas, but. What could your intention actually be? Could it be one word, a sentence, a paragraph, a philosophy? Let's see what other people think. My word for this year is compassion. I am declaring this the year of self-love for me.

Recognizing that I need to be compassionate. Towards my mind and body so that I can live my best life. But also practicing more compassion to others, cultivating new friendships. And nourishing the old through acts of compassion. Throughout the year. OK. Acts of compassion throughout the year. They want to live their best life, Of course. What is the best life might vary from person to person. What's the phrase? We lose our health, gaining wealth. We then lose our wealth to try and recover our health.

Whatever age you are now, are you under earning over earning? What's your work life balance? Are you overspending? Could you cut back on spending and have more time with your family, with your children, with yourself, with others, with causes, organizations, charities? We only have one life, probably. So what do you do with your 24 hours a day? Your intention could be to maximize the benefit of your 24 hours. The benefit to whom? Your animals, your friends, your neighbors, strangers, those dying of starvation, the other side of the world, you have to decide that for yourself.

Here's another intentioned idea that comes to mind. Is growth. So that's a one word intention. And what is that growth? Economic growth? Surely not material growth, surely not spiritual growth. I would have thought so. I would have thought that's what that person meant. Let's try another one. My word. Well, actually, the phrase is live well, I started focusing on this phrase last year. And it served me really well in 2016. This year, I hope to dig a little deeper into what it means for me to live. Well. OK, living well, well being spiritual wellness, mental wellness, physical wellness, does your wellness depend on how the people you're working from home? This Book? Well, this part of the Book is about self-care at home. So are you living well at home?

Do you have a separate space for your place of work, how you work in the ideal environment, if you've been on more than one of my Books, or maybe just this one? You realize I have different shooting environments to give you the viewer a different background, but also me as well, because when I shoot these chapters, I then go through them and edit them. And to be honest, just having the same background, same green screen or the same wall or the same sheet, or oh, just be boring. I know some people like that as a background. I don't. Having this type of thing. For me. It's useful. But a variety.

And if I were to pan this round, you see various other sets around, you can see behind me the Tibetan flags here. Because this is shot in a huge room. But sometimes I shoot in other rooms and sometimes I shoot downstairs. Sometimes I shoot out in the garden, sometimes I shoot when I'm walking on the streets or perhaps even along the beach. I have to be careful who's in the background on what they are wearing or what they're not wearing. Still, this is about self-care.

At home for home workers. So what about some intention phrases? Let me put some down in front of you. I just mentioned a couple, but you'll see quite a few going down to accept whatever happens as if I had chosen it. To develop a scale. And improve myself. Here's an exercise right down. Skills that you have and that you'd like to develop, not necessarily to get a better job. Speak five languages. Play the piano. Learn three types of programming. Learn lots of digital marketing exercises around the time to learn lots about digital marketing. So what about other skills like empathy or emotional quotient?

What about the scale for looking after yourself if you don't look after yourself, how can you look after others, but if you overindulge yourself, you won't be looking after others. Skill of tolerance, knowing when to let go. Knowing when to begin, knowing when to stop. To allow myself, Grace to follow the flow, to discover who I am and what I enjoy to be the person. My friends can rely on me. To find beauty in everything. Well, why not choose one of those or create your own? But hang on. Earlier, I quoted someone and they said that their intention was growth. And I said it could be spiritual, mental, physical or economic.

So maybe you'd like to focus on a single word for your intention. Okay. Put some more down. Peace. Joy, patients. Courage. Play. Simplicity, excitement, satisfaction. Family. Rest. Love delight. Passion may be more than one of those, maybe one of those every month. They are for you to do with what you will. But this chapter is simply about setting an intention as part of your self-care working at home, remember work life balance? The intention can be one for work and could be one for non-work or could just be one for the whole day or the week or the month of the year. It's your Book. It is up to you.

Doodle/Scribble

Welcome to this chapter. Previously, I was talking about intentions, remembering things like beauty, breathing empathy, excitement, satisfaction, family, rest, acceptance, self-care, which is what these chapters are about self-care for people working at home.

Peace. Peace in your work life. Even though you may be competing with others. But peace in your private life as well. Generosity, patience. Solitude. Wonder OK, let's take one of those words like peace papers, and let's take one of these words. And what I would like you to do is write the word in the center of the page. Any of those words, or maybe one that you've chosen for yourself? Let's set the mood almost as if it's just you and I in the same class.

Let's set the mood. OK, so here we have a rest , a sense of peace, slightly more golden lighting. And then I want you to scribble one continuous line around it without looking at your scribbling. So scribble one continuous line rounded, keep twisting, turning in and out, left and right. Just. Explore where the line would like to go, you start off like this with whatever the word is. I think your eyes, let's do this for I don't know. I can't, I can't.

I can set a timer for a minute. Let's see if we can do this. Just one minute. Just do it together for the eyes. It's now. Yeah, okay. So my eyes closed. Just go where the line wants to go. Whatever the intention is and overthink it. OK, that's hot in about 50 seconds or so. Well, what can one say in Typekit that? As you wish. You could say. And I certainly wasn't deliberately doing this. This is somewhat remembering the word is rest. If this is someone who is just lying down to sleep, maybe a bird lying down to sleep. Or you could say it's a whole being like a dog lying down to sleep. And those might be the ears and then the face, you might say. This is a pathway, and then it rests, curls up. Oops. Close up into a ball and then stop. So let's see if I add something, let's say. Could be. I have the bed, I have the dog, perhaps rest lack of movement, curvy lines.

I, Of course, didn't know that these were making what looks like a path. Maybe the pathway to rest. Or maybe it's a bird. Yeah. It's about to rest. Or maybe it's waiting for food, perhaps that's up to you, it's for you to experiment. This is about you finding things suitable for you, what you could do with your word of intention in the middle of the page. If you have one word of intention per week, put the word up with the drawing behind the wall behind you. It's just an idea.

This is all about your work environment at home because you're working from home. Office games are different. This is about self-care for you at home. Let's move on to the next chapter.

Grid

OK, the last two chapters have been about intention, remember putting the word here? One of the things you could do? Simple. I'm just going to use the back of this page to save paper, really. So let's say I divide it into two one two three three four six squares, let's say one week for each column. And I could have something like morning, lunchtime, evening or early morning, so early morning. So pre-work, work, work and evening.

I could have something like that. And therefore, I've got a grid in front of me and maybe doodle, this is doodling, not just doing one wavy line, but perhaps doodling. Yeah, I know that probably doesn't mean anything to you, but I know what it means to me. Let's be ahead on a platter, but it's not very good. But the point is you could do doodling now. No, you're working at home. So yes, it has worked here. But this is a sort of a three hour gap or three hour block.

You can take some time to do it or time to doodle and out time here. In the House that I share with others, there's one person who works from home and is supposed to finish at five or 5:30 to push. Often he's working till seven. I said, Why are you doing this? He said, Well, my boss kind of expects it from me. I said, If you're paying you? He said, Well, no, but I mean, I'm putting the extra effort and I don't have to go to work. I'm working from my room and I said, That's not the point. Do you enjoy your work? He said, Well, sometimes and sometimes not.

I said, if you weren't paid, but your rent was covered and your food and everything, so whatever your monetary needs are covered, would you still do the job? He said no. He's not doing it for the love of the job he's doing because he's getting paid and I like the job, but he wouldn't do it for free. So you need the evening to yourself. So if you're doing something like reading television or sports or cooking or walking or socializing, what you do, maybe not. You might do too, before you finally went to bed, perhaps. But then you build up over the week and perhaps your doodles would change. You could build in here.

Lunch, lunch break, not lunch break for doodling, but just a new timetable. But what you're doing is you're creating your own group and you're working from home. It's very, very important to have a routine. And in a way, this reminds you of your day if it's in four chapters. Because you have sleep as well, so let's say that this is 16 hours but late. I would suggest this is not for self-employed people. I'm talking about people who work from home and who are salaried. I would suggest that that shouldn't be more than eight hours.

Now you may well have been used to 10 hours a day if you had been commuting. So it's a bonus you've got time here for pre-work, which could be walking, socializing, not on the computer unless you're reading my Books, Of course, which are an admirable way to start the day. And here's your work block, and here's your lunch time as your doodles or your therapeutic type activity, drawing one line with your eyes shut, for example, or writing your intention in a block and here or. Different intentions. It's up to you. But the grid gives you a routine. That's the point. Like a timetable and routine, very important if you're working from home. Thank you.

Back to Childhood

Welcome to this chapter. I did think about showing you my desk, my little spotlights here and various pens here and paper and loads and loads of other things, more pens which have now fallen over and even at a fine for when things get a bit hot. And that's despite there being a lot of space all around. And this chapter is all about. Mess or being messy or painting. Like a child. So you're creating perhaps a background to an art journal or you're just engaging in activity, maybe you're working from home, but you have lunchtime, you have a pre-work time, you have a post.

What time? So why not regress? Remember what it's like to be a child, paint like a child and not talk about necessarily about what you actually paint and talk about how you paint? Don't give a—about all the mess parents are going to clean up. Well, if you work from home, it's probably going to be used as your own mess, but still OK. So how do you paint like a child? First of all, put on some sort of smock because you're going to get paint everywhere? No, I'm not going to show you get paint all over my white shirts and everything. So you put on a smock. Oh, T-shirt. Oh. Whatever, you're working from home. Come on, you can do this. Put on the smock. Grab a glass of juice cookie.

I'm not saying cookies are good for you, they're not. But when you're a child, you're probably brought up with cookies, so grab a cookie. But why not cut up an apple and have an apple instead? So juice or water would be better if you got some water, grab some water for yourself, a glass of sparkling water? Maybe. So grab some water, Apple, you got your smock and you're going to get messy. So you've now got painting material all around you. Here's your paint brush. Move your brush in a haphazard way. That means maybe your child. Oh, as in crisis, you bend the bristles.

Probably too much splashes in different places. You job at the paper. Your strokes are too heavy, but some are too light. You're not paying a lot of care and attention. Two reasons, first of all, your child. Secondly, this is your break in the day unless you're doing this early in the morning. What are you doing in the evening? Probably not. This is your relaxation. If you like in the middle of your day working at home, you've only got 45 minutes for a break.

Five 10 minutes get changed. You've got your material. You stored it up over there and a box in preparation for this. So you're working quickly. Airstrikes are too heavy. Sometimes they're too light. You're painting on a variety of different pages. You're going back and forth between different projects. But you pushed for time to go, 45 minutes to get yourself sorted, sort yourself into the activity out of the activity back into maybe office clothes if you got a Zoom meeting, at least the top half bent stand up. So you've got to allocate your time wisely. And when you finished.

In the break, in the break, you've allowed yourself in your work at home day when you finished, leave your supplies out. No, not directly in front of you, but maybe to the side to remind you of the break that you had to remind you of the activity where you painted like a child. And then, I mean, if you work in an office, you probably have a tea break. So providing you don't splash everywhere, maybe if you use paints, maybe now use felt tip pens just to add a touch here or there because you have a good time to put on your smoke and get your brushes and everything.

Just kind of add little bits because remember, it's the process, not the final product. That's important. So you finished one. It's now 3:30 time for a tea break. You can have a cup of tea. No, you can have some water, but. Yet the painting that you did three hours ago put it up with a few felt tips. So you're going back for a few minutes and something unexpected happens. You've tipped your water over your painting now, not your computer, we don't want anything to be too drastic. Not over your nice office clothes. Or maybe you've got some of the paint still wet.

It was only three hours ago that you did this. You didn't realize until you finished with all these pens that actually you had painted down here and here. Luckily, you're not at work, so you keep your hand hidden in your next meeting. Yes. And I think the marketing project for our worldwide development, if we consider development in Africa and we combine with our activities in Japan and China, take into account exchange rates and predictions. You can do all that you hit in your hand. You've hidden your hand with the paint on the paint that you got because accidentally.

You rested your hand on the wet paint that you created or that you spread in your lunchtime when you were painting like a child. And like a child, you had that enthusiasm like a child, you had to mess. And when you picked that up from the side and you would break like a child, you grabbed it and like a child, you were careless, careless, careless, careless. That's the background to your day, and also if you're painting and it's going to be an art journal when it dries, that's your back cloth. Thank you. Thank you.

Breathe...Draw...Breathe

Hi. Oh, all right. Yes, I'm breathing in deeply. One, four, six, eight methods. Well, yes. Breathe in for hold. Six Breathe out eight. Yes, that's fine. Well known for the 6th method or methods like that. Not that uncommon. Of all the techniques that I've learned and remedies that I've found that the women have gotten this positive feedback about, I've done it for probably 25 years and I really owe a lot of my health to that. So for those who haven't heard about it, will you explain how that works and how often you have to do it?

It's a very simple technique. Basically, it's breathing in quietly through your nose to account for holding your breath for a count of seven and blowing air out forcibly through your mouth to a canopy. And you repeat that for four breath cycles and you've got to do it at least twice a day religiously. And after a month, if you're comfortable, you can increase it to eight breath cycles. It's desirable to slow the whole thing down as you get familiar with it.

You can do it more often, but never more than four or eight cycles at a time. And the real effects become noticeable after about six weeks, six eight weeks of practice. It slows heart rate, lowers blood pressure, improves digestion, warms your hands, and it's the most effective in planning the stress measure I've ever found. All right, start by taking a breath out of your mouth, making it sound like a wash. So breathe all the air out of your lungs, starting now, breathing in with your nose and mouth closed. One two three four hold two three four five six seven Breathing out two three four five six seven eight one two three four hold two three four five six seven Breathing out two three four five six seven eight one two three four hold two three four five six seven Breathing out two three four five six seven eight one two three four hold two three four five six seven Breathing out two three four five six seven eight Breathing normally now opening your eyes when you're ready and repeating this twice a day presence is only a few breaths away and you need nothing outside of yourself to feel a little more grounded and to spread that to everyone around you.

But you're working from home, you can do that any time, but these chapters are about using art therapy or therapeutic activities. So what you could do is you could draw your breath so as you breathe in. You are drawing something with your pen or your paintbrush unlikely for working from home to the paint brush, but you probably got pens so as you breathe in the following breath. With your pen and when you exhale now, you can do this without looking down what you can do with looking down.

Remember, we're only concerned with the process. What we're doing is allowing the breathing in and breathing out the motion within you with the movement of your arm or your hand or the foul table to paintbrush. So when you exhale, you keep the pen or painting or drawing implemented. You keep it moving. But in a different direction, so you inhale, exhale, inhale. I exhale. So you're moving in different directions, and as you're doing this in time with your breathing, you know, deep breathing, you inhale.

And also, if you're holding your breath, you keep the paintbrush open, you keep it motionless. So as you inhale motionless and then exhale. Notice what thoughts arise and let them float by what you are focusing on, remember you're not looking at what you're doing, you just know that you're going a different way each time. You're not changing colors. So even if you are skilled enough to have two or three different pens in your hand and maybe the blue in and the green four out, you could try to draw both sides or use both at the same time.

Perhaps there'd be a parallel, but you're not so much focusing on that. You're focusing on the breath. So you start, say, with 10. And do that for, say, for three minutes. I mean, you're at work, you're working from home. How much time do you have? Can you afford five minutes? If you can't, perhaps there's something wrong with the way you're allocating your day. But what you could do when you've reached your time, when you've reached your goal time, well, when you've done your 10, 20, 30 breaths.

Forget that you're always going in a different direction. See what you've got, then you're now looking down. See what you've got in front of you. And then continued to draw, adding whatever inspires you. So what happens is what is determined, how long? Your line or your movements were two things. Well, three, if you count pressure, how fast you are letting your hand go, Of course, but how long your breath was as well, it wasn't determined by, Oh, I think I draw that for about three or four inches or I think I'll add that there, Of course, size of the paper, but you can get a three paper, sellotape it to your desk in front of you unless you're going a long way over the edge of the desk, which seems unlikely, then you're not going to overdo it. So therefore taking the assumption.

The speed of your hand doesn't change, your line is determined by the breath, and so therefore the line is your breath. And so what you have done is drawn your breath. Now at the end of this, you're continuing your drawing, but it is of your breath. No, it's not in a different cloud. You know, like in the speech bubble, you're not drawing it like that, but you are representing your breath with these lines. Plus the fact you're breathing in and out in a relaxed fashion. Steady movement. That by itself will relax you and who knows what you would come up with? Again, you're working from home again. You could end up, as I said, as I said in previous chapters, putting whatever you've done on the drawing of your breath. Round where you work. And the chances are that whatever you draw will be fairly peaceful, particularly if you're choosing peaceful light colors, and so you'll be creating a peaceful environment in which you work. Thank you.

Looking More Closely

Welcome to this chapter. This is very much like an exercise you may be familiar with mindfulness where you look at a raisin and you imagine it. What made it where it came from, how it grew, what it tastes like, how it feels. But you're working from home. These chapters are geared towards people who are working from home. So therefore you pick up something that's to do with your work, like in your little office, something. That's to do with your office environment. So if I take, for example, this. This is a spray. I used to clean glass.

I'll clean my glasses before I make these chapters. I'll leave these off for the moment because I'm not going to take up your time with me cleaning them. So where are you anyway? What you do is you take the object. Remember, it must be to do with your work, not a flower or a child's drawing. But perhaps the stapler, some paper clips and a mini fan up, a light and notepad, a calculator, a mouse, take the object, examine it closely. What does it feel like? There, and I've never read this.

I certainly can't read it without my glasses. I've never read the small print. But perhaps the object has a small print on it, where is it made? Does it say how long since you used it? Where did the materials come from? Where did the object come from? What sort of environment was it made in a factory? Or was it handcrafted? What's his function and could it serve any other functions if you were to design the product, would you design it like that? Is it too big or too small? Is there anything you could add to it to make it more useful? For example, it's just an example. If it was, say, a stapler, would it be helpful if it had a little pocket at the back to put spare staples?

Not many just say if you are down to your last tape instead of hunting around for a box or buying a new box, you've got 20 spare in the bag, just for example. Or, if it's, say, a container of pens. These are just examples. Would it help me at all if I had intentions or affirmations or logos, anything around the side? So what you're doing is you're looking at the object more closely.

- What is it to do?

- What is it made of?

- How does it help you?

- What would happen if you lost it?

- Does it need replacing?

- Where did you get it from?

- Where was it made?

- How long would it take to get?

- Could you buy it locally?

- Did you buy it locally?

- Was it imported?

- If you lose it, do you have a spare?

- If you did lose it, would it make much difference to your work life?

- Was it expensive?

Those sort of things. So you're looking at something that's in your work life. But mindfully and therefore gaining the benefits from it. Maybe it gives you ideas, ideas to make new products. That performs a similar function as well as a different function as well. In fact, new inventions or new products often come from people who are looking at an existing product and think that reminds me of, Oh yeah, that shape is similar to, oh, I wonder if that could be added to it.

I'll give you an example when you're traveling. You're going to different youth hostels, for example, different places, and you want to buy some bread, but you haven't got any butter, so you could buy a loaf of bread. Cut it up. Would you buy butter to go on it as well? Or probably?

- Would you eat it loose?

- What about those lipstick containers?

- What if or the ones you put in your lipstick as a prevention against getting chapped lips?

- What if you had those made with butter inside?

So you could spread them on and then they are enough to say four pieces of bread and then you dispose of them. They are on the market now, but 20 years ago they weren't. But they were in a joke book coaching Doku Shindo, who is the Japanese author of Making on Useless Inventions. If it happens to be raining outside, you could put on these shoes. And your feet won't get wet, but would you actually wear it in public? Probably not. Do you ever find yourself tired of having to use a butter knife to butter your toast? Just grab this stick of butter. It's never been easier. If it's not just your shoes you're worried about, but your entire body. Grab this umbrella when it's raining outside and you'll be covered from head to toe. If you're not sure whether or not it'll rain later in the day.

Grab this umbrella tie. The handle will be hidden away. And your style will be on point. Granted, if it's not raining, you can leave your wallet and your tie at home and wear this pocket tie with all your documents right at hand. You can also put your baby or your pet to work with these four mops. They're on the floor anyway. Why not? But this one might be your favorite when you have those tricky spots to reach on your back, and a friend is kind enough to offer you a little scratch, wear this shirt and use this guide to point them to exactly where it itches. We'll take it in.

And there's a whole series of inventions that were deemed to be totally impractical, and that one wasn't impractical. There was another one and I accept that this won't happen if you have a wooden floor and you get little gloves for your dog or your cat, and then as your dog, your kids round, it's polishing the floor. I'll put some up on screen for you to have a look at. Before getting engaged. Here we go. And that's it. That's all there is to it. Everybody, here we go. It's a brand new version of an embassy, go just off your feet and clap your hands and everybody is a hamster that mountain time do the. You don't even have to shake your brain. Be. Let's try it.

A Closer Look

Welcome to this chapter. This is really a follow on from the one previously I remember when I was looking at this. Admittedly, it was somewhat blurred and you've got your object, you've been looking at your object. OK, now put the object to one side. Remember, you've been looking at it closely. You've looked beneath the outside. You've thought about how it's made, where it was made, what it was made of, what it did, what the small print said, what its functions were, how it could be adapted now without looking down, but not as one continuous line, necessarily.

Just try drawing it, looking at the depth. Of what you actually felt and looked at more closely. So you are drawing what you've spent the last four or five minutes looking at very, very closely and thinking about, except you're not looking at it. And then see. What it shows you does it show you anything extra that perhaps you hadn't seen before and then when you've done that, next time you look at this, do you see anything in it that wasn't there before? Do you see perhaps what it was like before it was developed to this level? I mean, just for example, this is on the side of it. When I get off. Well, anyway, it has a cleaning cloth that comes with it, one of which is sold with that in the first place. It reminds me of a story of somebody who went to a toothpaste manufacturer and said, If you give me a percentage.

I can increase your profits dramatically. And they saw that, OK, what do we do? And he said widen the hole, the toothpaste, the toothpaste to come out, widen it for people, squeeze the same intensity most times, but more comes out the floor, so they use it more quickly, so they buy replacement more quickly. And somebody did something similar to one Vester match, you could strike the match from both sides of the match box, they said. Take one of the strips away and they said why reduce its functionality? And they said yes, exactly. And by reducing the functionality, that side gets worn out more quickly.

And so they have to buy more matches for the consumer, which actually in a way gets a poorer product, but blames design rather than anything else and so still buys one vest for the matches. Not very positive, that is it, so for this, how do you increase profits? Well, I suppose you could detach that to make this more colorful, perhaps, and then sell this separately on the grounds that you could have different types of this. So this is blue to match this. But maybe you could have these different colors, different patterns. So people always have character, they carry this with them and they also carry this. It's just an idea anyway. So what were you doing?

I've not cleaned my glasses. So what you are doing is drawing the object. You're not trying to be accurate because this is a mindfulness exercise. So you're drawing implements, let's say your pencil was like a little and that crawls across the page very, very slowly. And you'll find that you. It's not a fantasy to join because you're not looking down. You'll find that there's a lot more detail. Then you're drawing because you're going to draw things that you couldn't see before. Or you didn't see at first glance before and when you've done the drawings, I said, you then look back at the object and maybe it would look a bit different.

The point is it's a mindfulness exercise that you can do in your break or maybe even while you're working, while you're waiting for a phone call back and you're using something to do with work. Therefore, this is something that would change you working at home. And after you've done this, you'll look at this thing that is to do with work and you look at it slightly differently. Thank you.

Office Supplies

Welcome to this chapter. Previously, we've talked about drawing things, things that are all part of your office equipment, all pretty straightforward. This time I'd like you to get together a range of office supplies and just make art from them, particularly, say, with paper clips. Can you make a necklace?

With your paper clips, coloured paper clips, different colors, perhaps. Add color to them, but would it smudge your skin or your blouse or your shirt? Perhaps. Use a hole, punch or post of different colors. Blue paper, maybe create a collage, cut out different bits of your Post-it notes. And that staple them onto the paper or make different shapes and glue them on and create a collage of different interlocking circles, perhaps for different days.

Yes, you're not doing anything particularly productive. Your boss said, But you are doing something creative that helps distract you for the allotted time. Remember, I talked about grids for the allotted time away from work. Allowing you to relax and explore creativity and see what your college turns out like. Have some images? Thank you.

Working from Home Effectively

Working From Home is becoming increasingly popular, available and empowering! Imagine if you could work for any company in the world and not just those that are based in your city or country. Or imagine if you had more flexibility to care for your family, renovate your home, or start a business. Working From Home is a commonly misunderstood and understudied skill, but if done right it can truly transform your career and open a lot of new doors. Despite increasingly becoming a part of our everyday lives, amazingly, most people are never taught how to be effective in making your own schedule and workspace. So, in this Book, you'll be walked through step by step on how to simply and effectively manage your time and space at home, regardless of your industry and personality type.

This Book covers everything you need to know about running a Home Business, working in Virtual Teams, or even Working Abroad. Essentially any situation where you might need to spend a day at home instead of in an office building, but still be productive, focused, organized and Of course happy. We focus on extremely practical actionable changes you can make to ensure Working From Home is just as effective as working in an office... Perhaps even more! You'll learn whether a daily routine is truly essential, tech and tools to make life easier, mastering virtual calls (as a guest or a host) and creating a brilliant office space at home. Say goodbye to feeling low energy, distracted and unmotivated, and instead enjoy the simplicity of building your own schedule. This Book covers detailed tips for excellent planning using Gantt Charts and PERT diagrams, managing a team, avoiding overspend, predicting risks and dealing with multiple stakeholders.

After this Book, you will feel calm, collected, well prepared and confident that you can work effectively from anywhere. You'll know how to create your own schedule and find your own motivation and goals. We look at lots of real-life software and set up examples and give you practical tools you can use right away to get better results in your day. Whether you're a solopreneur with a home business, or part of global virtual teams this Book will empower you as someone who is always one step ahead.

By becoming productive and effective at Working From Home, not only will you pave the way for a future promotion, but you'll also have transformed your own personal happiness and freedom potential!

Introduction

Welcome to this news chapter on mental health at the workplace. Art therapy and this whole aim of this Book is to improve your workplace existence. But what about actually having enjoyment? And that's the purpose of this chapter. We're going to be going through 13 office games.

Also, there will be office games, known ways of improving office well-being being shown down the side of the screen as I'm talking. So at the end of this, you'll have 13 games, which may be tried in the office, but you might lose your job. But anyway, you may try these and Of course, lots of other ways to improve your well-being and health

at the workplace.

Doing A Wheelie

So oftentimes let's try the first one, the first one is called doing a really doing a wheelie. For example, you take an office chair, I'm sitting in an office chair now. And if you look at sales pitches for office chairs or wheelchairs, people talk about how comfortable they are. I can raise the seat.

You can lean back quite happily. You can have a backrest on and attach things on and and all that. What they don't emphasize is how smoothly they can be pushed, the acceleration, the torque, or even how you can push them around corners at high speed. And those are the important things, surely for office games. So doing a wheelie or having an office chair derby is what it sounds like.

Can you push someone in the chair at high speed round the office and they're sitting there with their feet up in the air as if on a motorbike we lift the wheel up. You could even depend on the wheels on the chair. You could even try it with some of the wheels off the ground. Now, Of course, what you really need is a route not just unplanned around the office. You need some obstacles, perhaps like a kink in the carpet, or maybe a few telephone lines, or maybe some books left carelessly on the ground.

So if you move a few desks, you can create a racetrack and you know where the office printer is or the office photocopier. That's the hairpin bend. And in fact, you could even encase one of the wheels. Certainly one of the wheels comes off these chairs that I've got here. You lift up and the wheel comes off. You could if you're doing wheelies and maybe the wheel will come off so you could actually have a pit stop next to the water cooler.

You can have a sweepstake as to who's going to win. It can be done at lunchtime or after work or before work. Or maybe. And this is why you might lose your job when the office manager is not there. You could have a chart up on the wall who's going the fastest. You could even bring in special oil for the wheels, perhaps, or choose your running mate or your sitting mate based on their ability to lift their legs up in the air quickly without falling out of the chair or based on how heavy they are or how easy they are to push. So that's your first office game doing a wheelie?

You Aren't What You Don't Eat

Welcome to office game number two. Assuming you still got your job, this one is called You are what you don't eat now. Many offices or many work, canteen or work, eating or factories give out healthy food. You have a vegetarian option, a vegan option, and perhaps you can no longer eat pork. Or perhaps you cut down on your saturated fat. Or perhaps you have somebody who comes into work every day with their own packed lunch.

It's the same as yesterday's because they prepare in advance in their slow cooker at home over the weekend, and they bring in perhaps their low carb or carb free lunch every day. It's a sandwich without the bread. Hmm. Anyway, they have their low carb lunch or no carb lunch, and they put it in the same spot in the fridge and they have it in a nice sort of Tupperware box. So what you do is get your own Tupperware box and you take it in turns to switch the boxes around, assuming that they are the same.

I'm not talking about you. Open that Tupperware box, take out the food and put in a burger. No, I'm not saying that hygiene. Where do you store that food? Come on. This is just a game. We don't want enmity. We don't want fisticuffs at the office. You just swap. And so they go to what they think is their Tupperware box.

Open it up and there's their superfood. Salad has been replaced by an old burger, perhaps or anything with high saturated fat.

And remember, this is your Tupperware box, but you've changed it over. You could even leave in a little Post-it note or buy one of these pads. Just buy one of these pads and leave a note something along long, leave a proverb, perhaps you are what you don't eat or or leave it saying or just a message saying your food was so healthy, I thought I'd replace it with something else, or this was very nice. Could you perhaps put a little more salt in it?

Now, the person who wins this game is the person who doesn't get sacked, the person who doesn't get hit by the person whose lunch you're constantly changing, or the person who's not identified as being the originator or the creator of the idea, or the person is not identified as switching or actually caught switching. Perhaps it's best done as a team, perhaps as for you switching that poor one person's food, so they prepared.

All you need is a lunch box. The same as theirs, a distraction for that person, access to the fridge and some sort of self-control. As that person takes out, the lunch box goes to their desk, puts it down already to eat their vegan salad or whatever opens up. There's a grizzly burger. Who did that? Everybody else is over their computer and they're busy working and inside. They're screaming with laughter. So that's the game, you are what you don't eat.

You Have A Message

Welcome to this office game very violently, and this one is cold. You have a message now, often when you find someone that's a pre-recorded answer phone message, perhaps on their voicemail, for example. So you do need access to their phone or their company phone. And while they are away from their desk, perhaps they're taking a day off that day off sick or days off.

You managed to get access to the answer phone message and you changed it. Now you don't change it, so it would cause a bad reputation for the company. We don't put something on it like, I'm lonely, please meet me at 10 o'clock in the car park. You don't put something like that. It's got to be funny without causing wow. Without causing too much damage. Certainly, you don't put something on like, don't buy from this company.

The products are rubbish. No, no, no, no. I'm not suggesting that what you could do is put something on that might just be real. Something like, I'm sorry, I'm not at my desk at the moment. I've had so many hoax phone calls. Would you please preface your message with the name of your favorite vegetable and say to someone? Here's that. And leaves the matches like a carrot. This is Georgia marketing, thank you for the advertisement that you placed to you. I was £10000 or this is Sally from consumer research. But instead of saying This is Sally from Consumer Research, we get a banana. This is Sally from Consumer Research. That's if it's a fruit or if it's a fruit, vegetable or anything, really, but nothing that is damaging.

Now, with a game, you've got to have a loser. I think I think we have that person, but you've also got to have a winner. Well, as with other games, the winner is the person who does not get caught. Now, remember, the person whose phone it is just might end up listening to the answer for a message. To find out why people are saying my name, Stanley Banana, Fred Carrot, George Broccoli. Susan Orange or whatever they might end up listening to their own answer, phone message, and then they might recognize your voice. So what you do is you disguise your voice. Perhaps even impersonate somebody else.

Now, if you could impersonate somebody who is not part of the game and that person gets blamed. That's even better. Or if you could impersonate, was this a bit risky? Perhaps if you could impersonate the office manager or the company director? Not naming anybody. Just impersonating. So if the person whose answer phone has been. Distorted then blames the office manager. Well, even better, or is that too evil a game? It's an idea. Imagine how you would feel, not if it was done on you, but if you're done on somebody else and you hear what's happening, someone comes in.

Been away for a few days and then they go to their phone. Oh, they've got three messages beat. And they hear the first message, and it's a potato. This is Derek from finance, we have a few queries over your accounts. The. Brussels sprouts. This is Susan from production. We have to talk to you about stock levels or beep carrots and so on, that's if it's vegetables or orange or bananas or pears or whatever or different types of cheeses, for example, entirely up to you can actually even vary it. We've had so many hoax calls. Please leave the name of the fruit.

Unfortunately, we're being besieged by hackers. Please leave the name of your favorite TV program, that type of thing. See how long you can get away with it. In fact, you may even play with one another. So you can make it the funniest. Or if somebody leaves their mobile phone, their private mobile phone on their desk, even better, then it's more fun without causing any potential damage to the company's reputation. Play with it.

Bulls**t Bingo

Years ago, when I used to run business at these seminars at schools, we used to play something called—bingo. So you give out cards with, say things on it like marketing makes pricing, packaging promotion, people place market research, advertising after sales service, product life cycle extension strategies and you give a card out to each pupil.

And then when the chapter or teacher launched into jargon like blue sky thinking or low hanging fruit, things like that. Or you can try a whole load of new words from this website, then that tick it off and then the teacher chapter wouldn't know about this. And then at the end, whoever got the bingo, the lines of all were, let's say, bingo, anybody for that with laughter and hopefully the teachers would say, What are you talking about? And then you tell the teacher or chapter what was happening?

Well, you could do the same thing at work, couldn't you? You're going to a meeting and you give each person as they go in, perhaps secretly a bingo card with phrases or aphorisms that the person giving the meeting is fond of saying, Oh, it's talking about I'm a bell shaped curve or extrapolated data or smoothing out the sombrero. Those, Of course, are from recent newscasts, perhaps phrases like going forward, so strategic staircase or brand actualization. And whoever wins ticks off a line they can't shout.

And can you give us three ways of extending the customer approach to the company going for bingo? You can't really shout that out in the meeting, but what they could do is have a sign where they go like that, perhaps or like that with something not expected. If they're right-handed, they use the left hand to poke their ear so that people know or they could make it a little bit more difficult. They have to interrupt. When they've got the bingo, they have to interrupt whoever is speaking. That's a very good point.

But whatever it is, and I have to interrupt the speaker and then develop that point, that makes it more difficult. But it also means when they say, Oh, I have to just interrupt you, but everybody else knows what they're talking about.—bingo. Give it a try.

Hovering Around

Welcome to this chapter, this office game. This is quite tricky. This is called hovering around and really you don't want to be caught doing this, so it's probably best to do this when the office manager or supervisor is not there because it'd be difficult to explain. You can hardly say. Well, I was trying to swat that fly or I was just testing the speed of the wheelchairs or something. This is more obviously some sort of game. OK. They're in the office everywhere. That's everywhere, on computers, everywhere.

You imagine that the carpet has somehow got electric charges running through it, the sort of accelerated global warming, if you like. Therefore, you cannot touch the carpet. Or perhaps there's an under carpet alarm system. And if you touch the carpet. Cage shutters would come down overall the doors and you'll be stuck there for the rest of the millennium. The important thing is instead of walking round the desks to get to the printer, the toilet at the water cooler, to go for lunch or whatever, you've got to be able to do it without touching the carpet at all.

Therefore, if you mustn't touch the ground with your feet, how do you get there where you could walk with your hands? Could you really walk all that way with your hands? It's quite difficult, but if it's going to put pressure on the alarms, if it's electrified carpet, that wouldn't work, would it? Luckily, the chairs are insulated as the wheels. But hang on. How do you prepare yourself? That's for you to try and figure out. You could perhaps stick to the desks so you're crawling on one desk and crawling onto the next. It depends how close you are with all this social distancing or physical distancing. Oh, you must wear your mask because you're going to get hot and sweaty, so perhaps you crawl over people's desks.

But what happens when you get to the destination, the kitchen, the photocopier and the printer? What about when you go to the toilet? What if you're imagining that the toilet floor is electrified or any pressure was set off the alarms? How do you use the toilet without your feet touching the ground? It's all very well if you use the sit down toilet seat to sit down with your feet off the ground. That's fine. But how do you get off the toilet or even a toilet seat? Well, how do you even get to the toilet?

Somebody else carries, you know, you can't do that because their feet touch the ground. OK, someone else is in a chair push. They managed to propel that chair into the toilet. You're sitting on their lap, you jump off to latch onto the toilet seat. But do you really want to sit on someone's lap and go off to the toilet together? Maybe not. Anyway, this game is called hovering around, so you're hovering over the carpet. If you haven't got a carpet, imagine that there is a carpet.

If it doesn't flow, imagine there's somehow pressure sensors there that keep you occupied, right? Do any work but keep you occupied. Loads of fun reduces stress. You must have all these arguments prepared. Remember, and in case the court enhances wellbeing, leads to bonding more teamwork.

LAUGHTER is a stress killer. Improves productivity, makes the place a much better place to work for. Boost morale.

Improves company image because workers are happy. Employees are happy. Reduces labor turnover. All those sorts of things. Get them ready. Because if you're caught, it's going to be quite difficult to explain.

Limbo Lunacy

Welcome to this chapter on office games now. I remember when I was involved with the theater company Second Voice Players. I went to one of their drama evenings and one of the exercises we had to do. We had to walk around the room, or we imagined that we were walking over ice and there's invisible string or between. It was held in a church between the various pillars, and the string was at different heights.

And this was all to improve our balance and stage awareness and also as an ice breaker ice breaker. We were all nice straight as an ice breaker because as some new members in the group. And so therefore we'd walk around bending and weaving because of the invisible string. In effect, we became limber dancers. And so this game is called limber lunacy. So you imagine, for example, if you have two filing cabinets.

Well, two desks or two dividers between desks and at the early stages, just when I get used to, I think I fit, you're going to become. You have a string tied between the two filing cabinets or between the two desks or dividers, whatever you're imagining this, I don't need any props. And it's at the waist height of the tallest person in the office because we don't want to start off with it too difficult.

And therefore, every time you walk through, you have to go under that string. And everybody in the game has to obey these rules, if you don't, you've lost the game. No harm done. No way this has any uncomfortable situations in the toilet. Other people who are not involved in the game may wonder what on earth is going on. You could tell them you can charge them an entrance fee to the game. You could have other pieces of string. So these two here. So for example, here's your two pillars. Then you have a third one over here.

For example, you've now got three. And at different heights, and these can be set by the person whose turn it is to organize the game, remember, it's all invisible, so there's not much organizing. And perhaps this time the limbo line could be the waist height of the shortest person in the woman in the office. Then you can add a rule that the string is not there only between certain times of the day, like it's not there between two and three. One minute past three.

If you go straight through, you've broken the string, you've lost the game. Go that five to three. No labor dancing whatsoever, you can just walk straight through and everything is fine. Or perhaps you could have the string going up six inches every hour or down six inches every hour, so by five to five in the evening you're prepared to go home. It's not only two feet off the ground, you've lost the game if you can't get under the two feet. And obviously, this is limber lunacy.

You don't fall over. A fun game. Easy to organize. No props involved. A bit of attention to detail, but not much. Now if you can go through all of this. Otherwise, you're going under the string and people not in the game. Don't ask you what you're doing. Then you can be the overall super super winner. So you've not only managed to get under the string, but you've managed to do it without people realizing what's happening now.

You might then say, Well, this is just an example of how people ignored me in the office. Or you might say this is an example of how hard people work in the office, concentrating so much they don't realize what's going on. This is all your defense in case you're caught. Now, if there is a winner in all of this, there must be some sort of prize. The winner, remember, is the person who manages to get under the changing limbo string and non-players in the office.

Although once you've done this once, I think everybody in the office would realize what's going on. But non-players don't challenge that person. They don't notice him or her, or they just think it's a bit odd. Is there some sort of smell between those two cabinets? Or you could even perhaps put a little red tape or red marker on other cabinets. And when its red string is there, when it's blue, it's not necessary to put it in different places in the office as you develop the game and become more and more aware. So the winner at the end of the day and of the week, what are they? What prize can you give them?

Alter Ego

Welcome to this office game. Very straightforward, no one's going to get into trouble. I hope to remember there's various tips going down the side of the screen as well. All right. Let us assume for the purpose of this game that the four of you play and, you know, loads about football or, you know, loads of lyrics, many lyrics to songs in the chart, so or not. Or you are familiar with slogans or you're very familiar with quotations or you're very familiar with the thoughts of various philosophers.

Anything that you will all know what the other person is talking about. So let's say we're talking about lyrics and you know that such and such a singer, one of the most famous lyrics are this. And somebody else is a different singer. The famous lyric Is this so before a meeting discussion you allocate? Perhaps you have a. Mug on your desk and you put in the names of various stars, as in pop stars, they take out the name just before they go in and nobody knows who is who. And then during the meeting, they must somehow be in the discussion.

And you can do the same with anagrams. Somehow, in the discussion I put in a line from one of the lyrics. And the winner is the first person to be identified, they're all too eager to be identified. So for example, if, let's say, the manager is talking about, well, we've had an increase in sales of five percent over the last quarter, but in products A, B and C, there's only been going forward. There's only been a marginal increase of two percent. Can anybody suggest ways in which we can increase sales of that product? So you put up your hand and you say,

Well, what you've got to do is look at that particular product and imagine that you are in fact, that product. And so you are now that product. I'm a survivor.

And so therefore you improve the quality of the product, which means you're going to be able to sell more of the product, perhaps raise prices depending on what competitors do and what the markup is. But if you notice in that little rant that I put in the phrase, I'm a survivor. And because I said, I'm a survivor, you, the other game player might recognize I've taken on the persona of Bounce, say, for example. Now I have chosen the lyric, Well, I've chosen that line for the purposes of this chapter. But what you could do is the day before the meeting and there's five of you playing.

Give out five names with some lyrics with those names. But remember, you don't know who you're going to be taking the name at random. So you might recognize it in somebody else. So what are the difficulties? The difficulty is in remembering the line from the lyric. The second difficulty is in putting that line into the meeting at a relevant place. The third difficulty is recognizing somebody else if they manage to put in their line for their persona in the meeting. Try it. It's quite fun.

Planting Evidence

Welcome to this office game, I really should have loads of office plants around me to make it more like an office where all the hair is fresh and the view is fine and so on. Plants and this game is called planting evidence, and it's very, very high risk. I was watching an episode of Friends recently, and there's a case when Rachel said that she had shown her assistant mail assistant reports. He said he'd never seen it. And she found it on her desk. So she then, when he was away, put it in his drawer so she could later accuse him of having had the report all the time.

He then discovered it and managed to put it on her desk when she was away. And so when she accused him, he opened a drawer, said, No, I haven't got it. She's confused. She goes back into her office and then finds it on her desk where it was in the first place. So this is similar. So your task and I say this is risky. This is very risky. When your manager. Oh, this assumes he hasn't got a clean desk, a clear desk. When he's away, you go into his office, you take something off his desk that is not incredibly important, so you don't take his mask off. And obviously not be a bit tricky. But for example, let's say he has a low depends on his desk, and let's say he has a pair of scissors as well, something that sticks out from the others you take.

In this example, you take his pair of scissors and you put it on your desk. Hidden. Now. If you are caught. What are you going to do? Admits it was a game? You'll be disciplined. You could say somebody else put it there to frame you. And unless it's closed circuit TV everywhere, they're going to get away with that. Now, if you are really evil, you could put that pair of scissors on somebody else's desk, hide it on their desk. And the winner is the person who gets most of that desk onto somebody else's desk for the longest period.

You've got to be careful to put it on someone else's desk. Are you bullying them? Are you discriminating? Perhaps it's better to put it on your own desk and then claim somebody else put it there. Now I said scissors, because that's different from the others. I think if you took a pencil off, they probably wouldn't notice the red pen. Well, would they? Would they really notice, perhaps as these pens are different. But if it's not there, they just use another pen. But if the scissors are not there and they need them every day, for example, then that causes. Slight amount of inconvenience, also perhaps bright yellow, is it more difficult to hide on your desk, perhaps as company scissors? Of course, you could be really brave and take the whole lot and hide it behind the office plant that is on your desk. Enjoy.

Round Robin Rubbish

Welcome to this office game in general. Although you'd better think about it, you could lose your job, self-respect, and friends. So be careful. This game is called round robin rubbish. It does rely on people opening their emails almost immediately, they get one, perhaps WhatsApp would be better, not text.

Just be careful because you'd be using your email or WhatsApp for non-business activity. But let's assume you have a waste bin that is for everybody. And it's the same distance from, say, four of you sort of a central West Point, and the game is you send the email around to your three game players subject title or rubbish. Or the subject title is important so that they read it. And then one word rubbish. But the point is, as soon as they see the word rubbish.

Well, you could use a different word: throw or game on or play or now something that's agreed. Perhaps if it's a work email, you could just put the word urgent with a question mark and then put genuine text underneath like. Sorry to bother you, but I'm not sure what day the holidays are, and I'm doing the holiday rota or what time is the meeting I need to know. Just in case you're caught, but because you put, say, three question marks, which is the agreed sign.

People, people know really what your email means, so they open up the urgent three question marks or or rubbish or now and immediately they see it, they've got to take whatever they've got to hand like to pen or if it's a if it's a piece of paper, whatever piece of paper they've got to hand stood up and throw it in the bin. So if this works, you would see within seconds of sending the email or the email could be sent by a third party that is not part of the game. They send the email and then for no obvious reason.

Suddenly four people grab the piece of paper they've got and check it in the bin and the winner is the first person to get the screwed up paper into the pen, not near the pen, actually in the bin. So let's say this for if you're doing this and the fifth person who sends the email and you're watching, try to imagine this in your mind. You're watching this happen, you're busy working. And then suddenly four people pick up a piece of paper and chuck it in the bin for no apparent reason. These odd occurrences happen in the office or in school, perhaps. But in the office, you do have to have a central bin. But what you could do perhaps is put a spare waste bin somewhere. Um, there's a leak in the ceiling or you have to have some reason for putting it there. I'm just asking you to visualize it and how much fun this could be. Round robin or rubbish?

Vanity Publishing

Welcome to this team. This is called vanity publishing. Now you may have seen advertisements, sometimes I'm contacted by people. Would I like to enter this poetry competition? And you send off your poem with your face for £10, $10 or 10 euros and your poem wins. Because it appears in this volume of poetry, you're very pleased. Oh, by the way, if you want to buy the volume, that's another $20.

So really, you spent $30 and got your poem published, hence vanity publishing. This is similar. I suppose you get a photograph of one of the people in your office. Perhaps it's on Facebook or a company prospectus or it's up on a wall somewhere, or perhaps you've taken a photo of them, or perhaps it's a photograph on their desk which you've then photographed. You then go to the photocopier and you photocopy it, say, 100 times.

Probably the photocopy has a built-in camera so that management knows what is being photocopied so that they know you're always doing work related to photocopying. And you photocopy, say, 100 pictures of this person. It's not you, by the way, you don't distribute them, you just photocopy them all. Of course, you could print them out from the office printer. Now that person is then held over the coals by his or her manager, why did you do this? Why 100 copies of your photograph sitting at the desk or the one that you've got on your desk? Well, maybe not 100.

Maybe just five copies are enough to cause a ripple. That person, Of course, would say it wasn't him or her. But this is the game: who did it and why? Well, I can't really answer why it's a game, but the game is. To be anonymous, not to be caught doing it. So, yes, the photocopies or printing is locked. Yes, the guilty party is identified supposedly as the person in the picture. But you've got to be careful, particularly if it's printing. When you go to pick it up, you're not caught.

If, Of course you are called, then the person you've been taking the pictures of photocopy in the picture, printing the picture of is going to be furious. And that could lead to disciplinary action. Also, you've clearly been wasting his time at office facilities. Sackable offense. First warning. Second warning. So the trick is not to get caught. Now you might say this is a dangerous game. It's irresponsible for me to even suggest it. No, it's irresponsible of you to accept it or to try it out.

Perhaps you could do it with just three copies. And leave them lying around somewhere nowhere, you know, not telephone boxes and saying phone me for liaisons, just leave them lying around on a desk. Why is my photograph being copied? What is the picture of me doing there? Nothing nasty, you know, in the toilets or anything like that. That's nasty. That's bullying. And no, I'm not suggesting that.

But you could, for example, pin one on the back of the person's jail, stick it on the BlueTEC. They would know next time they got up. No harm done. Just one copy or two copies or they go off to the toilets, come back and there's a copy on their chair, on their desk, where did it come from? How did they get that picture? That's the fun. So these games are for fun and not for damage or malevolent behavior. They're not for damaging the company's reputation, and they're certainly not forgetting you or anybody else.

Overheard Over Here

Welcome to this brief chapter of his games proving mental health team, bonding fun at work, not wasting too much time or money, bringing a little levity to the workplace atmosphere. It's your choice, whether you do any of these, these are just games. This one is called overheard. Over here now. You pick up the phone. Hello. Yes. X-Y-Z Corporation. Can I help you? Yes, we do have those in stock. Oh, you're having to return three of them. Are you? OK, thank you.

Thank you very much. Could I interest you in this product? You've now got two choices because it's called head over here. If they say thank you goodbye and then put the phone down without you having to say goodbye, what you could then do because other people can hear. It pretends that you are continuing with the conversation. So, yes, we have some more in stock. And they say, thank you. Goodbye. People don't hear you, hear them say that. So you say, yes, we have some more in stock.

No, I don't want your phone. I'm sorry. It's against company policy to accept your phone. Oh, you live in the same area. Yes. Well, I suppose we could meet up, but are you married? That type of thing. And then at the end, as people have stopped their work and they're listening because I actually that's not real conversation. Be careful, though, because quite often company phone calls are recorded so your customers are putting down. The phone hasn't stopped the recording and so you are still being recorded. Now, some of the house could do, no, it's called overheard over here if you could let the caller, the person who's calling into your office, think that they are hearing the end of a shocking, ongoing conversation in the office before you greet them. So imagine that this is my phone. It rings.

I pick it up, but instead of immediately saying hello, can I, can I help you or thank you for returning my call? If it's called a display or X-Y-Z Publications LtdI pick up the phone so they ring a ring. And if you are caught with that, you are going to be. Hello. Good afternoon, sir. Can I help you? Or so you've been pregnant? Good afternoon, sir. So they think they're overhearing some sort of conversation and the winner is the person who gets away with the most outrageous comment. So somebody rings. Yes, we've got print or something else. So your son's going to cheat in the A-level dice?

Absolutely. Good afternoon, madam. Can I help you? So the winner is the person who doesn't get into trouble with his employers. Of course, he doesn't get the customer telling them off. He doesn't get the customer slamming the phone down. He doesn't get the customer complaining to your supervisor or the person who makes the most outrageous comment without being challenged. Now, Of course, to protect yourself, you might like to write up this game before you actually do it, saying last week this was tried out in the office and it was tremendous fun in the company newsletter before you actually do it or even tweets about it. So you could see one of the guys we have in our offices to do this, people say, Oh, that's really funny.

And then you go and do it. But by then people might be aware that it's a game, so there's less likely to be damage to you or to the company or the company reputation. Clearly, you don't want to make it too realistic. So the phone foundry, what five people have died from the virus this morning in our offices? No, not something like that, but something like, say. Your dog or your lunch? That's permissible. So be sensible with these games. The aim is to have fun without causing damage, without the serious expense of anybody else. Most importantly, without being at any huge cost to you. Thank you.

Sweet Success

Welcome to this office game. It's called sweet success. Have you ever eaten love hearts that have a little message like, I've always loved you. You are the flower of my heart or my heart beats faster every time. Every time you walk by you, by a tube of love hearts and you bring them in. But you don't tell anybody, except there other people playing in the game, obviously, but they don't know that you're the one with the love hearts. And the aim is to leave a message.

The love heart on the desks of non-playing co workers. So the non-players, oh what? Somebody just you are the love of my heart. I love you more. Every day, darling, blow me a kiss. Each day I come to work. It is for you. I mean, you can make these notes up, but don't have to bring in love hearts. But the idea is to leave it on a non playing person's desk. And the winner so you can have five of you playing your Monday, Tuesday, Wednesday, Thursday, Friday and the winner is the last person to be caught. So if you are creative art therapy, et cetera, you could even decorate these little messages.

Not too much, because if you do too good a job and you're a good artist, people, it's you. And the point is not to get caught. That's why if you buy a tube of love hearts, then nobody's going to recognize your style of drawing or handwriting, whatever. And the whole idea? Leave it on someone's desk. They go away to lunch or break, or they're out of the office, so they come back. Or or not, they may not eat. That's not the point. And Of course, you're watching it, or maybe you can't see them having lunch together. You know, somebody left love on my desk this morning.

Got any ideas? Oh really, sir. What did it say? Oh, it said my true love question mark. Renee, I've got it. Was Gladys over there? Or. Or maybe George over there? I've watched that type of thing. But again, if the fun becomes too serious, if, for example, the person who's picked up the love heart as a rail with George because you've suggested it was George when it wasn't, it was you. Then you gotta be careful that the fun only ever is fun. No damage to anybody, and certainly no bullying. These are just games you could just play amongst yourselves.

And again, be creative with the note that you leave with a love heart or perhaps leave a cucumber on the desk. And guess who? Or banana or potato or broccoli and anything? The game is not to get caught. So you pulled a day out of the hat manager and said, Set aside Friday and you pick out Wednesday, for example. Nobody knows your Wednesday. They know they're not Wednesday, but they don't talk to each other. I mean, I'm Thursday, so obviously it's not me leaving the broccoli or the potato, the decorated potato. Let's get creative. So I know it's not me.

I know it's one of you. Four, But I don't know which one, and I don't know when it was left. That would be much safer. And if it's something like a vegetable or fruit or or even, let's say, I don't know, let's say you had a comb and you just leave a message on the top. I've come to the Earth looking for you. Or can I be the lead in your pencil, which you sell to the pencil and you leave on the participating players desk when they're away? Be as creative as you like. It's certainly fun. No one, if it's participating players. No one is harmed. That's the point. You've had fun. No one's lost out. Think about it.

Clip On Art

Welcome to this chapter. This is called Clip on Art. Paper clips, this is what you do. I mean, assuming you've got paper clips of work or if you're working at home, at home and the game is to make the longest paperclip chain, you can stretch across the office or between desks or between dividers, between desks or waste paper bins or anything like that in the shortest time.

So you've only got a break, for example, you've all got a bright 10 minute break, or you're more likely you've got a lunch or lunch break. And it's to see if you can make the longest one in time, or you could add on a bed. The most attractive one if you've got different colored paper clips. So the winner could be the one who makes the most attractive change or the most original run like origami or perhaps wear as a necklace at a meeting different colored paper clips. And the winner is you wear to the meeting, and no one says that's a bit odd. Oh, what the hell are you doing or why are you wearing that?

Did you make that at work? Who knows? Christmas is coming. Perhaps you could sell these as necklaces or if you run your own business. What about branded paper clips or perhaps paper clips then attached to something else like a name badge or a logo? Be inventive, creative. This harms no one and is quite fun, but do it in your break, then spend hours at work. What are you doing? Oh, I saw this about office games that improves mental health and teamwork and bonding and good for image and reduces labor turnover. Yeah.

Have you answered those emails? Well, now I've been making this paper clip. No, no, no. Do it in your spare time. So the contest is to be the most creative, the most colorful, the most attractive chain, or perhaps the longest or in the time you could. Send an email, aren't participating players assuming people have a notification on their laptop or whatever? And it just has one lined paper clip. And as soon as you see that you've got five minutes to make it so suddenly for five minutes, three of you put down tools and paper and they go to wet round the neck.

And the winner is what with the most clips or the best necklace, all you have to design your own rules. That's the great thing about these games. You can interpret them or twist them or add on bits or to duck bits as you wish. This is James. You have paper clips of work, which is a reasonable assumption. If you do this, pose some pictures. Question answer chapter. Let me know how you get on. Thank you.

Master Hiring & Interview Skills for Recruiting the Best Fit

Are you tired of struggling with hiring and worrying about interviews? Do you want to recruit the best talent and avoid the costly mistakes of making wrong hires? Look no further than "Master Hiring & Interview Skills for Recruiting the Best Fit," a transformative online Book designed to equip you with the essential skills and techniques to excel in the hiring process.

The importance of finding the right talent cannot be overstated. A bad hire not only costs you tremendous amounts of money, time, and effort but also has a significant negative impact on your company and yourself. That's why it's crucial to master the art of hiring and interviewing to ensure you make the right decisions from the start.

This Book is your guide to becoming a master in the hiring and interview process, regardless of your level of experience or background. Whether you're a new beginner or a non-HR professional, you can learn and master these skills. In fact, the skills and techniques covered in this Book are applicable not only to hiring but also to your daily life and workplace situations. You'll discover how to apply them in conversations, business meetings, staff coaching, projects, team collaboration, and more.

Don't miss this opportunity to transform your hiring and interview skills. Enroll in the Book now and unlock the secrets to recruiting the best fit candidates. Start your journey towards becoming a master of hiring and interviewing today!

Thank you for choosing our Book.

Introduction To The Book

Hello and welcome to the expert academy and to this effective job descriptions Book here together we will cover the essential elements for crafting high quality job descriptions and give you specific insights on how to write them, well equipped with the tools required to align your job descriptions with role expectations and teach you how best to attract high quality recruits. Maybe your recruiter, a human resources professional, the head of a department, part of an external communications team, or maybe you are an office administrator no matter what your role or level is at an organization.

This Book will help you to feel more confident in the way you produce job descriptions. During the short Book, you will learn how to compose targeted and comprehensive job descriptions, how to attract the best people to apply for the post, and how to recruit the best talent for your organization. Perhaps you've already had some experience writing job descriptions and have run into some challenges. Maybe you have questions about what information or how much to include in a job description. It could even be that some employees in your organization don't understand their role because their job description was inadequate.

So you want to rectify this and avoid it happening again. Maybe you are anxious about legal ramifications associated with an inaccurate job description. Perhaps your job descriptions are outdated and need an overhaul. Or maybe you're just trying to attract different types of talent to your organization. All of these are real problems for you and your organization. But don't worry, we hear you and we've got it all covered. You've taken that all important first step and recognize the issues surrounding job descriptions. And even more importantly, you enrolled in this Book.

Together, we will tackle these problems and will find answers to your questions. So by the end of the Book, you will feel ready to rework, reimagine and revitalize the job descriptions in your workplace. You will learn through a series of short video based chapters and put your learning into practice through downloadable activities and tasks. You will also be supported by our job descriptions writing guide, which you can keep by your side for a reference.

You see, I told you we have it all covered. So let's look at what is in store for you after this introductory chapter. Our second chapter will look at what a job description is. It is important, after all, that you have a secure knowledge of what you are trying to achieve when putting a job description together. In addition to that, we will examine different reasons for needing a job description and who is responsible for writing it. In the third and fourth chapter, you will learn what the fundamental components of a job description are and the functions of these components.

By this, I mean that we will discuss the structure of a job description, the key elements to include and how a well written job description is going to help you and make your organization more productive. Now, that is quite a promise, but if you think about it in the building trade, if you have good foundations, you're going to have a solid house. Well, it's the same with job descriptions. If you nail the structural process, laying down good foundations and getting those key components right, strong results and talent will follow. And it is that stand out talent that you want in your organization. Right?

In the fifth chapter, we will look in detail at the process of writing a job description. So you have a clear picture of the steps to take as well as what content to include. And we're going to do some demystifying, too. We'll show you exactly how to make your job descriptions appealing to millennials and GenZE demographics. They're not new species. They're just human, but they are motivated by particular things and driven by a different outlook on life. It will all be revealed later. Importantly, we will allow you some of the pitfalls of writing a job description, what not to include, how to use unbiased language, and how getting the balance right between sufficient detail and access is really important.

After all, it's so much better to be forewarned and forearmed than suffering the consequences of badly or erroneously written job descriptions. All of this will be covered in the sick chapter. The seventh chapter explores who to call upon to write a job description. The great news is that you are not going to complete this process by yourself to write the most effective job description. You are going to need to collaborate, use new ideas and revise accordingly. It's always good to get more than one perspective in life.

After all, in the eighth chapter you will learn how to use the job description in recruiting where and how to post a job vacancy. Specifically, we will explore the difference. Between a job post and a job description and how each day is used in the recruiting process, we've also got some great advice about where to effectively advertise your job vacancies, what to include in a job post, and how to make it dynamic and stand out from the crowd in the penultimate chapter. We will look at the long term, what to do with your job description. Once you've hired your talent, you will learn how to use the job description to help the new recruit set goals and meet expectations in your organization.

You will also see how to use a job description as a framework for employee reviews and create transparency in the review process. And then it's the final chapter and a chance to recap and consolidate your learning and obviously a chance to give yourself a well-deserved pat on the back for your hard work and also a chance to recognize those fresh new skills you've acquired, which you're going to be putting into practice in the workplace. So now you have an understanding of what we are going to cover in this Book, I hope you are ready to get going.

It is good to remember that by taking the initiative and enrolling in this Book, you have shown that you understand how important it is to get a job description right and are ready to put in the time and effort to gain new skills to do so. So let's crack on and begin by discussing what a job description is and what it does.

What Is A Job Description?

So what exactly is a job description then? Let's start by giving you a clear definition of a job description. A job description is a written document that clearly outlines the functions and requirements of each position in your organization. So our key words here are clearly functions and requirements. Remember those?

I'll be referring to them again in a later chapter. And another important question to ask is why do you need a job description? A job description is not only absolutely essential in the hiring process, but it's also critically important for setting expectations of each role in your organization. Having a solid job description in place can help you evaluate whether expectations are being met and thus can help you plan for the future needs. Moreover, a job description helps guide the interview process and can serve as a kind of competency matrix for your employee reviews.

In fact, a well written job description can remain with each employee throughout their time in the company. Another crucial role a job description plays is in keeping morale up and retaining staff in the organization. This is because it sets clear expectations for employees. It's only fair that each person in your organization has a roadmap for how to succeed, and this roadmap takes the form of a well crafted job description.

Now, if you are responsible for any hiring activities in your company, including recruiting or interviewing, you are probably pretty familiar with the functions of a job description, which we will discuss more in the next chapter. But maybe you're a manager or a supervisor currently outsourcing your job descriptions to an external recruitment human resources agency and wondering why you're not attracting the talent you want. Don't worry, we'll teach you what you need to know to review and revise job descriptions that land on your desk before they make it onto the job board or into an offer letter.

If you want to invest in a good resource, there is a lot of useful information about job descriptions in the Job Descriptions Handbook Third Edition by Margie Maida Clark. You'll be delighted to know that we've done the hard work for you and squeezed some of it and its themes and key points throughout the chapter series. One final note. While this Book can and will benefit anyone who works with job descriptions, keep in mind that there may be certain requirements for government related positions or union workplaces as we won't be exploring these specialized situations in this Book, you should check for any prescribed guidelines before crafting job descriptions in these types of special circumstances.

Great. That is the first introductory chapter completed. You now understand what a job description is, some of its purposes and the role it plays in the recruitment and retention of staff. With this knowledge secure in your toolkit, you are already well on the way to writing an effective job description. So let's move on to chapter two and talk about the fundamental components and functions of a job description. In the next chapter, you will learn about the function of a job description.

The Function Of A Job Description

What do you think is the most important function of a job description? Most people think of a job description just as a hiring document or a recruiting tool. In fact, a well written job description can stay with an employee throughout their time at the company, serving as a reference point for their role. It can guide recruitment managers through the interview process.

It can and should be included in an offer, letter or employment contract. It can even help form an orientation checklist when a new employee joins the company. What a lot of professionals find is that job descriptions can also act as an organizational system. With the system in place, departments ensure all responsibilities are covered and that the correct number of roles exist for the work that needs doing. Does that sound like a worthwhile benefit? I can see you nodding in agreement through the screen. Another important function to mention, and though we hope this never happens in your organization, is that legal teams can reference job descriptions in the case of discrimination or wrongful termination claims.

So if you haven't got the picture yet, the job description is a really, really important document. Just a minute. Let's go back and clarify some basic definitions so we know a job description is a comprehensive document that clearly defines the functions and requirements of a position. However, this should not be confused with a job post. A job post is a public advertisement with the purpose of attracting talent and ultimately filling a position with a qualified candidate. Therefore, a job description should include much more detail than a shed in a job post, though the two can certainly share a lot of content. We'll talk more about job posts in a later chapter.

One of the most useful and even fun aspects of writing job descriptions is that the exercise allows department heads to identify skills gaps in an organization. All too often, managers get bogged down in their day to day duties and forget that they may not have the right skills on their team to achieve department or organizational goals. Sound familiar? For this reason, it is a really good idea to pin down department heads and managers across the organization and make them write down job descriptions for every role on their team.

Whether it's already filled, it's open and needs to be filled or it doesn't even exist yet. You may be imagining all the resistance you will get at the suggestion, but let me point out why it's so important in doing this. Task managers should think about the current state of their team and their collective and individual skill sets. What's lacking are all these missing pieces able to be distributed amongst the existing roles, or are they substantial enough for a new role to be created? By going through the process of writing a job description, departments and recruitment managers can identify any changes they want to make at the organization.

For instance, your organization might be migrating from a manual system to an automatic system, and that requires a completely different skill set. Or you might be wanting to incorporate new digital tools and technology. And you need someone who's already well versed in these programs by defining these qualifications up front. The department heads not only make your life easier, but will avoid the cost and time and commitment it takes to train a new employee to learn these new skills. It's also worth remembering that job descriptions will vary across industries, as will the length and content of each chapter.

For example, some job descriptions like those in health care or academia, will probably require some very specialized skills. So the chapters that list necessary expertise will likely be more technical listings and specific degrees or certifications. Other types of industries like sales or marketing might include technical education and certifications, too, but the chapters addressing expertise may emphasize certain industry benchmarks or quotas met. And the importance of these requirements will also vary across industries.

For example, a certain degree might be absolutely mandatory to perform a role in engineering, while recruitment managers in the tech sector might be more concerned with a candidate's experience rather than their advanced degrees. In general, though, job descriptions will list a combination of hard skills and soft skills. OK, you have now learned about the functions of job descriptions and you should be able to see how your organization can best use a job description in your workplace. Download the activity for this chapter and put your learning to the test. You will find that you are really getting to grips with the basics to help you tackle the task of writing job descriptions. Next, we are going to look more closely at the individual components that make up a job description.

The Components Of The Description

So what are the components of a job description?It's time to get into the nuts and bolts of the structure of a job description. While there might be some variations, depending on the industry or sector you're in. You will find that most job descriptions include the same kinds of detail. First, there's the job title. This needs to be specific. It should accurately reflect the primary job function.

It should also use language that reflects the level of seniority of the role. For example, a proposal coordinator is going to have fewer responsibilities and a lower salary in comparison to a proposal manager. A marketing specialist is going to describe a very different type of role than a director of marketing and so forth. After that, you might want to consider including the department and supervisor beneath the job title. For instance, the job title for a benefits administrator might include Department Human Resources.

The job title of a software developer might list the department of it and report to the director of computer services. The next part to write is the job summary. This is a short paragraph that serves as a kind of opening statement for the job description. It needs to provide a brief and compelling description of the job. You can think of this chapter as the elevator pitch, a couple of sentences that sum the role up that can be easily communicated to someone within the time it takes to open a lift or an elevator.

Following on from the job summary is the essential function chapter. This should be a thorough numbered or bulleted list of all duties required within the role in general. Listed items are easier to read and remember the long paragraphs, so we recommend using a list. The best way to phrase these responsibilities is by starting with a specific, actionable verb. For example, supervise and train operations staff, analyze incoming data and create basic descriptions, perform regular audits of all marketing collateral and develop new material as needed. Don't worry if this is sounding bossy.

This is just a clear way to express the job functions. And it is really important to be clear and accurate here as this is the chapter often referenced in wrongful termination lawsuits. This last chapter is often the job requirements and qualifications chapter, and depending on the role, this could be one comprehensive chapter or several more specific chapters. For instance, you might have a small subchapter dedicated to education that lists requirements for degrees, licenses or certifications or another subchapter listing skills like ability to operate heavy machinery or knowledge of best practices in accounting.

Regardless of what layout you choose, the job requirements and qualifications chapter should list both hard and soft skills and really be as specific as possible. So you'll need to include things like thorough knowledge of industry preferred database software, as as well as the ability to work independently. Think of this chapter as your wish list for your ideal candidate, but it is important to focus on which abilities the person should possess for the job and not go into personality type. It should include the type of professional background and skill set you are seeking in this person. And no, it is absolutely OK to mention which requirements and qualifications are required versus preferred if you're feeling a bit nervous about treading the fine line here.

Don't worry, we'll look at this more in the next chapter and give you more information to make sure you don't veer off that line. We are keeping you safe in this Book. And finally, below this chapter, you can include any additional information, for example, in a full job description. This is where you should list salary or salary range plus or benefits. There you go. You have now learned how to lay out a job description and the different chapters you should include to write it comprehensively, download our template as a further reference and start the suggested activity.

With this knowledge, you will now confidently be able to start to compose a professional job description yourself in the next chapter. We will examine the process of getting the right information for the content of the job description. First of all, we will look at the best language to use as well as the different angles you could take to present the role and attract the best candidates. Are you ready? Let's carry on then.

Key Focus Areas

OK, so now you are aware of the main components to include in the job description, it's time to investigate some of the best practices for your job descriptions, content. One thing I would really like to emphasize is to make sure that every sentence earns its place in the job description you want to avoid, including irrelevant details. Not only will the job description seem unfocused and unprofessional, but it might even discourage candidates from applying.

This is particularly common when talking about the candidate's personality. It might be tempting to include something like a warm and friendly attitude is a must. But ask yourself whether this is an absolute essential for the job. If a candidate doesn't identify as warm or friendly, they might not even apply. Even if they're highly skilled and able to do the job well. It is much better to keep your content focused on the role and ensure that everything listed is indeed necessary for the employee to do the job well.

For instance, excellent customer service skills are required as an example of a way to phrase this requirement because it's skills based rather than personality based. So to be really clear here, stick to the skills and not personality traits. Furthermore, you really need to use clear, concise language in your job descriptions. You see, I told you we would come back to this point. It might be tempting to fill a job description with the latest industry jargon or buzzwords, but it is best avoided.

However, the key thing is to ensure that your job description is readable and understandable for all job seekers.

You should also be specific about job functions, but don't overdo it. There's no need to list every single report. This person will ever be responsible for writing or every customer service issue that they might encounter. Find ways to sum up the responsibilities succinctly, like handle external communications with stakeholders as needed, or resolve any customer conflicts quickly and professionally. But what you absolutely must list is anything candidates should know about the physical aspect of the job. For instance, in roles relating to operating machinery, the job description should state clearly what machinery is involved in the role. In the same vein, you need to be realistic in your expectations about a role.

Don't ask that an employee be available 24/7 or be able to drive a truck for 30 hours straight unless you are looking to fill a superhero role that is seriously realistic. That said, it is also important to be transparent about the role if the job requires an employee to work a 12 hour shift, specify that in the job description. Another point to remember is that it is essential to be honest about the role of the company. This is crucial from both an ethical and a legal standpoint. If you advertise and hire someone for a position that ends up being drastically different from the job description, you could be facing some major issues down the line, not to mention exodus of your best employees.

Another thing to think about, if you are writing a job description for a position with no chance of rising through the ranks, don't mention possibilities for promotion. And if you're writing a job description for an entry level role that requires a lot of thankless labor, don't puff it up, so to speak, and exaggerate the duties. As you keep these things in mind, remember to use positive language that reflects your professionalism while we are discussing the types of things to include in your job description. Let's talk about your audience. Studies show that by 2025, millennials, by that I mean those born somewhere between the early 80s and mid 90s will compromise 75 percent of the global workforce and GenZE or those born somewhere between the mid 90s and early 2010s, a hot on their heels.

So this is something you need to bear in mind when defining the roles within your company. These two demographics are looking for very different things when it comes to job hunting than the generations before them. The first thing that is important to know is that research has shown that millennials are not necessarily going to settle in a job for life. They are flexible and ready to explore opportunities in different companies looking for the best job to suit. Then, from a retention standpoint, you'll want to know how to keep this group of employees satisfied.

Millennials top factors when deciding to accept a job or salary, work, life balance and career growth opportunities. Millennials are motivated by things like the opportunity to work from home, a flexible working day and plenty of paid holiday. Generally, they expect a pension and they are increasingly interested in maternity and paternity and benefits. In other words, millennials are looking for jobs that support and don't infringe on their chosen lifestyles. And moving on to GenZE this generation is similar in. Seeking that work life balance, but is far more concerned with the type of work they'll be doing as the most civically engaged generation on the planet right now. They tend to be very opposed to the work that could be considered meaningless or even detrimental to the earth or society at large.

In this case, the job requirement chapter is the place where you should try to use language that shows that the role is worthwhile. This younger generation also wants comprehensive benefits and paid holiday, but financial security is key as well. So if your company is trying to appeal to GenZE, you might consider implementing student loan repayment and tuition reimbursement programs. So there you have it. I agree there is a lot to take on board when composing your job description from using the best language to having knowledge of the scope and technicalities of the role to also having an understanding of what makes your prospective candidates tick.

But now you know, all of these points, you are in a great position to write with these focuses in the forefront of your mind and get the right candidate for the job well done in the next chapter. We will talk about those murky pitfalls you want to avoid when writing a job description. Are you ready? Let's get to them.

Pitfalls To Avoid

All right, we have discussed the components of a job description and what you should include. Now let's talk through what not to include. Here are some pitfalls that are all too common in job descriptions today in order to attract high quality talent. Avoid these at all costs, first and foremost, never include discriminatory language of any kind. While this seems like common sense, discrimination in job adverts or descriptions is surprisingly common and often unintentional.

It should go without saying that specifying a preference for any race, ethnicity, age, religion or gender in a job description is illegal. Let's say that again, specifying a preference for any race, ethnicity, age, religion or gender in a job description is legal. And I'm sure that you agree with me that underlying this point is imperative. One caveat here is that there are situations where candidates from a certain racial or ethnic background are encouraged to imply because they are currently underrepresented in the organization or at certain job levels.

For example, some police forces attempt in their recruitment to match the ethnicity of their employees with local populations. If you're in special circumstances like this, it's a good idea to have a legal team review your job description before it's made public. As far as gender neutrality in a job description goes, avoiding this can be tough. That's because unconscious bias can come through in coded language. There are gender coded lists accessible on the Internet, so you can check your job descriptions against them. For example, terms like active, decisive and dominant or masculine coded words, while terms like agreeable, empathetic and pleasant or feminine coded words.

The best way to avoid these pitfalls is to keep your job description focused on function and skill rather than personality type. Another thing to avoid is exaggeration and extreme modifiers. There's no need for job titles like data, rock star, recruiting ninja or marketing wizard. By the same token, don't describe your team as the best of the best or the ultimate perfectionists. Similarly, stay away from cliches. If you want someone to take initiative on projects, start one of your bullet points with taking initiative on projects rather than requesting a go getter.

While you might think this kind of language is more marketable, it's actually less accessible for candidates and could turn away high quality talent if they don't identify with these descriptors. Be accurate, professional and specific throughout the entire job description. That is going to be the winning formula for you and your organization. On the other hand, don't leave your job descriptions with formality or jargon which unnecessarily complicates things. This can make your organization seem stuffy, pretentious or out of touch.

A qualified candidate should be able to comprehend everything outlined in the job description. If there are highly technical responsibilities, listen, but don't include difficult language for the sake of a more intellectual sounding job description and always refer to the organization as we are the employee or candidate as you, rather than using third person language as we've discussed, be specific in your job descriptions, especially when it comes to the essential functions and the job requirements and qualifications.

chapters defining a role as being a jack of all trades doesn't really describe what is expected. Instead of listing overseas marketing teams, which are very broad, and manage to direct reports of a graphic designer and a social media coordinator, your employees should have a clear idea what the role entails with no false pretenses. I should also point out that there are some words which are best avoided as they convey negativity and hostility. Terms like Never Can't, shouldn't and must suggest an environment where the employee can expect to take orders rather than contribute to the work at hand.

Phrases like strict policy and difficult clients are not appealing and a job description probably doesn't reflect your company the way you want them to. And then just when you think you have finished your masterpiece, I'm going to tell you you haven't. It needs to be checked. Such a crucial part of the process and one that you may be tempted to sidestep if there is a deadline looming to make sure it is clear and concise, it's a good idea to run it past an impartial internal employee in a different department who has minimal to no knowledge of the role. If that employee can understand the job description, you're on the right track.

Finally run it through a platform like family to check for spelling and grammatical errors. Nothing looks worse. And a job description full of mistakes and typos. So there are a few things to be mindful of when writing a job description, using language that is non-discriminatory and gender neutral, as well as avoiding over-the-top cliched phrases and pretentious jargon. It is better to focus on putting things across in a positive, professional way and always remember to get the copy checked and proofread by colleagues. But now you are aware of these points.

You are better prepared for your task and you are well on your way to becoming a confident writer of job descriptions. Is that a round of applause I hear? Well, it should be great stuff. In the next chapter we will look more closely at who to include in the process of drafting a job description. Getting input from those around you will certainly make the job description more thorough and it will ease your load as well. Let's move on.

Who To Include In The Process

So who exactly should be involved in the process of writing a job description? Well, you will be delighted to hear that it is not your sole responsibility. You know, it is a relief job. Descriptions, as you can probably tell by now, are more important and complex than a basic summary of duties. A lot is riding on your job descriptions from the caliber of talent you attract to what's at stake during the interview and negotiation processes to the Longer-Term legal ramifications.

And then remember, job descriptions help identify gaps in teams and in the organization as a whole. Identifying these gaps can lead to changes in strategy, which can affect new recruits and existing employees, workload and distribution of duties, accounting and budget management and more. I'm not telling you all of this to scare you, but just to emphasize that the responsibility of writing a job description is too great to be placed on one person's shoulders. So we need to call on some additional support in the process before you even start writing the job description.

Gather input from anyone who will interact with the position you are documenting. A helpful exercise is to look at an organization chart and determine who in the company will rely on this position in some way, from superiors to colleagues to direct reports. Each person is going to bring a unique perspective on what they need from the employee in this role. When you request input from others, ask for a list of essential functions of the role, but also include questions like how is success defined in your department or on your team?

How will this job support your role in the company? And what strengths would someone in this role bring to benefit the team as a whole? This will help you understand the role holistically and then you will be in the best place to craft the job responsibilities and qualifications chapter of the job description. While it's a good idea to gather input from various people, ultimately remember that you want to keep the job description reasonable. The drafting process is where you'll need to use discretion to determine which functions and responsibilities should be part of the job description and what falls under the nice to have umbrella and is better left out of the document.

Once the job description is drafted, it's time to review and revise. Now, it may not be feasible for every person you gathered input from to also review the job description draft. So pick a few key people who will be working closely with this employee to read and give feedback. It's helpful to include a list with a couple of questions when you distribute the draft, like does this summary capture the essence of the role? Does this job description sound both realistic and appealing? And are there any significant functions or responsibilities I've left out? Giving you a review is a reasonable amount of time to read and respond to your request, but be sure to include a deadline so that you don't hold up the hiring process if applicable, once you've incorporated edits and suggestions from your final draft through your legal and H.R. departments to ensure that you haven't missed anything that could harm you later on.

Keep in mind that a job description is not legally binding unless it's included in the contract of employment. With all of these people involved in the process, you should be prepared for several drafts to be drawn on the job description. It is useful to manage these drafts by naming and organizing files appropriately. Even after the job description is finalized. You still want to review it on an annual basis, so keep it somewhere you can access it later. Another point is to remember that the role might fundamentally change over time, depending on the employee filling the position, the needs of the team and the business goals of the organization. If you don't keep your job descriptions updated, they could end up working against you.

So if the job functions or requirements change at all, or you find a skill set that fits the role better than the one you've described in the job description, you'll need to update the document. The same goes for any new technology that you require. The person in this role to have knowledge of regularly updating your job descriptions will keep your organization in compliance legally, as well as making future hiring much more streamlined. As you can see, getting others on board with writing the job descriptions is not only going to make your life easier, but it will also ensure you hire the right person for the relevant departments in your organization.

So before you get cracking with writing, think carefully about who you will ask assistance from, what questions you will prompt them with and what time frame you will ask for feedback. Once you are happy with the draft, you will need to pass it by H.R. or your legal department and finally make sure you file everything carefully for later reviews and updates.

Feeling confident now? You should be, as you've now covered the first three chapters of the Book. Well done. In the next chapter and next chapter we would attack. In her job, descriptions and job posts fit in the recruiting process, as well as some tips on where to advertise.

How To Post A Job Description

Where and how should you advertise your vacant role? This is what we will be looking at in this chapter, so we have spent a lot of time looking at job descriptions and now, you know quite how comprehensive they are and how many different components there are in one. In contrast, a job post, as we previously touched on, serves a different purpose.

A job post is essentially an advertisement for the position. And much like product advertising, its goal is to attract high quality talent and entice them to apply for the role. But this is a tricky thing to do, as I will explain. You see, researchers from job search firm The Ladder's found that job seekers spend an average of just forty nine point seven seconds before dismissing a post as a poor fit and just over a minute reading job adverts that appeared to match their interests or skill sets. That doesn't sound long, does it?

So how should you make your job post stand out amongst the thousands on a job search website? Let's take a look at some pointers to help you answer this question. First things first. A full job description for the role should always be written before creating a job post. The role must be clearly defined and documented in order for a smooth clear-cut hiring process to take place. If the extent of the role is not documented in the job description, recruitment managers will have trouble writing the advertisement to find the perfect candidate for the job.

And candidates who pose questions about the role during interviewing may find that the answers they get are confusing or inconsistent if the job description isn't clearly and fully defined. In fact, writing the job description up front makes pulling together a job post significantly easier. It also helps guide the interview process, since questions can be formulated directly from the description. So when it is time for you to advertise a position, you want to remember that you are marketing this role and it doesn't matter where you're marketing it.

Job search sites, online college boards, professional networking groups or social media platforms. The aims are always the same, attracting high quality talent for the position and encouraging them to apply. And what does a job posting include? Well, the job post would include a couple of things that the job description may not start a high level overview of the organization that markets it to potential candidates. While this might change slightly from role to role. It's a good idea to have a standard boilerplate outline you can use across all of your job posts for consistency.

Standard language will also help you from reinventing the wheel every time you need to post a new job. One thing you will have to remember is to appeal to Millennials and GenZE in your company overview. That means you need to mention any environmental initiatives you engage in, any philanthropy you support, and what applicants can expect. As far as flexibility and work life balance. Company culture is important for both of these generations. So include language in your overview about anything that they can expect in this regard, will they have access to an onsite Jim? Does the team do Friday happy hours?

Be sure to mention these in your job advert. And what about salary information? While the full job description should always include specifics about salary and benefits, a job post may or may not advertise this. In some sectors, this information is required to be listed. While other sectors may opt to leave this out of job posts. Some industries or positions have fixed remuneration packages, whilst others may allow for a lot more negotiation during the hiring process. So use both your discretion and the industry standard when deciding whether or not to include remuneration details in your job posts. But if you choose to leave this out, make sure you have a good reason for it. Keep in mind that many job seekers use filters on job sites to narrow their search results.

If you don't lift the salary range, your position could get messed up by candidates also including remuneration information, demonstrating that your company is transparent and it increases the likelihood that candidates who already have a job will take the time to apply if it's in their target range. Finally, you'll also want to include any specifics about how to apply. For instance, state your preferred method and format supplemental materials the candidates should include or a contact person for that cover letter. You can also mention anticipated interviews or start dates if you'd like. And then we come to where to advertise.

The most used free job boards in the UK are indeed monster guardian jobs read and Glassdoor. Social networking sites like

LinkedIn and Facebook generally act as supplements to help get the word out about a new job post in the US. Popular job board sites include indeed Monster CareerBuilder and snacker job Google for Jobs acts as a search engine across these various sites, and LinkedIn and Facebook are also heavily utilized for job posts. And how long should you keep your advert up for a while, you want to create urgency around the position.

Don't take it down too soon. Sometimes recruitment managers leave posts up for one or two weeks, but that's not nearly enough time for candidates to find you. We recommend leaving posts up for around 30 days unless the job is filled before then. One of the best ways you can attract potential candidates in the 21st century is to include video or interactive media in your doorposts. Remember, you are trying to sell the job to the best candidate. Having the business owner or an executive member record a video is the perfect way to share information through an engaging medium. It's a more dynamic experience for the job seeker, and it brings the organization to life.

Having said that, you generally shouldn't use video for the more specific components of a job description like responsibilities or qualifications. This type of multimedia is best used to highlight company culture and share the organization's core values through storytelling. Just be sure to always test it out from the users perspective on any platform you choose. If a video doesn't work on a certain site, you will need to include more written content. Now, at the end of this chapter, let's recap a job post is a marketing tool to help you attract the best candidates for the job vacancy.

It should include a company overview as well as specific information about the role, but may or may not include salary details. You should also make sure that you have included information that candidates will need to send in their application and specify any application requirements, give you a job advert, enough time to be seen and don't take it down too soon. And bear in mind those younger generations you want to attract to fill your vacancies, make sure you have sold your company in the best way you could consider, including video to give a dynamic experience to your potential candidates. Got it. Great. That's another chapter completed.

Make sure you have downloaded the resources for this chapter and completed the activities set to reinforce your learning. Are you ready for this final chapter? Fabulous. Now we need to think about translating your first class job descriptions into a high quality hire. This next chapter will look at how to do just this.

High-Quality Job Descriptions = High-Quality Hires

Is a job description just for the hiring process? Not at all. You can get so much more out of a job description. And in this chapter, we will explore all the possibilities. After you have recruited an employee specifically, we will be talking about how you can use a job description to shape an employee's orientation into a new role and how you can use it to review an employee's performance. Let's look at a scenario.

You have had great success at recruiting an outstanding person for a role, and they are ready to get started and dazzle you with their talents. But where should they start? They may be talented, but that doesn't mean that they know everything they need to know about the job or the organization. You will need to guide them and introduce them to the ways of your organization and the nitty gritty of their role. And this is where the job description can help you out by serving as a structure for the orientation

process.

For instance, you might break the essential functions and job responsibilities chapter into different chunks and assign timelines and benchmarks for the employees orientation to the company. You could make a list of what you expect the employee to accomplish within a certain time period. For instance, one list could be within the first 30 days you, the employee, will have bulleted items that they'll be expected to learn in their first month. You can dedicate the next list to expectations for the first 90 days, then for the first six months. But each time building on the functions and requirements stated in your job description, you could also use the bullets in your job description to set milestones in your orientation process.

For example, you might use a list item of build and measurably grow sales to set goals like within the first six months, the employee will build and measurably grow sales at five percent increase. What else can you use your job description for after recruitment? Well, most companies have a way of measuring employee success at their organization, often in the form of performance reviews. Whether this is something that happens quarterly or annually at your company, you can still use a job description as the foundation for the review.

When putting together a performance appraisal document, use the original job description to determine what to include. The job description, if written well, will encompass all of the competencies expected from the role. Perhaps your performance appraisal can list the bulleted items from your essential functions and job responsibilities chapters with a rating scale of one to five. You can start by having the employee write their own performance in meeting each expectation Then the manager can add their ratings as well before having a focus discussion with the employee in their review or appraisal meeting.

This also helps keep performance reviews from wandering into uncharted or illegal territory. In order for the conversation to remain legal, ethical and professional, the performance review should focus on how well the employee is performing each of their responsibilities. While there are other ways to address interpersonal conflicts and H.R. representatives should be present for this conversation. Using the job description as a basis for performance reviews keeps the conversation focused on how well the employee is meeting. That clearly defined expectations.

As you can see, if you have a well thought out and carefully put together job description in place, it can help you with other H.R. functions, such as orientation, goal setting and performance reviews for employees. It also allows employees to remain professional with each other. If employees are sure about the nature and scope of their colleagues' roles, this should lead to a harmonious and effective working environment. Now that is a Win-Win situation to strive towards. And so we are now at the culmination of the effective job descriptions. In this chapter, you have learned how to take a job description beyond the hiring process and use it to guide and assess the performance of employees in an organization well done for completing this fifth chapter of the Book.

Now you should grab the downloadable learning resources and implement the points. We have talked about orientation, goal setting and performance reviews in the set activities and there is just one chapter left for you to complete. You have worked so hard to reach the end of this Book and you have shown commitment and dedication to succeed. I salute you. Let's conclude this Book then, shall we?

Conclusion

Wow, we have covered a lot in our town together. We started off by exploring the many functions of job descriptions and why writing them is so important. We talked about how different people at an organization use a job description in different ways. We define the different components of job description and investigate each of them closely to determine what kind of content to include and what to leave out. We touched on the various legal ramifications involved with job descriptions. Then we looked at who to include in the writing and revising processes.

We discussed where to publish job posts and how to use video media in them. We talked about how to use a job description in your performance reviews. By this time you will hopefully feel as if you have learned a lot. Give ourselves a pat on the back for completing this Book and equipping yourself with some very important new skills. We also want to encourage you to make good use of the downloadable materials included at the end of each chapter. These are here for you to keep and reference regularly.

As you know by now, writing job descriptions is never a static process, but rather is always evolving. As you review and revise your job descriptions and create new teams and roles at your organization, you'll want to look back at what you've learned here and put it into practice. We hope you feel more confident about writing job descriptions than you did at the start of this Book. Remember that there is power in reviewing. So continue to write and revise, write and revise until you feel your job description accurately communicates what you want to convey.

Congratulations for making it to the end of this Book and thank you for joining us on this learning journey. We are cheering you on as you practice crafting effective job descriptions for your organization and attract the type of talent that your team needs and wants. We have a whole catalog, of course, available, so be sure to check out the categories and topics relevant to you and your organization. Best wishes from the expert academy and good luck.

https://www.udemy.com/Book/time-management-mastery-boost-productivity-and-save-time/learn/lecture/24064846?start=0#overview[1]

---

1. https://www.udemy.com/course/time-management-mastery-boost-productivity-and-save-time/learn/lecture/24064846?start=0#overview

Basics of Counseling and Career Counseling For Beginners

Counseling is a process of professional help by experts for individuals to understand themselves, to gain awareness, to identify problems and to produce solutions, to make decisions, to be in harmony and healthy communication with the environment. Career Counseling is specifically focused on a person's career opportunities, most often provided in educational, work, and some community settings. It also may have the specific goal of enabling a person to change the direction of his or her career.

The counseling will take account of an individual's preferences, intelligence, skill sets, work values, and experience. Such counseling is offered to groups as well as individuals. This course has been carefully designed to provide you with all the information required about basics of counseling and career counseling.

Introduction

Counseling. Interaction counseling that means charge no force no advice counsel it is nonjudgmental confidential changing counseling can help you work out what change you can make and how responsive the individual needs listening. Having time to talk to someone who isn't understanding to help you make sense of what is happening in your life. Definition of counseling.

Webster's Dictionary counseling is consultation mutual interchange of opinions deliberating together. According to James mutually. And it's manual G. Pattern counsel is a relationship between two persons in which one of them attempts to seize the other. In so organizing himself as to attain a particular form of happiness adjustment to life station are in short self a true allegation counseling always involves one to one relationship that is once silent and one ingredient will occur in a formal or an informal interview station.

According to Carl Rogers, a series of direct contacts with individuals which aims to offer him assistance in changing keys attitude and behavior really and Andrew counseling is a mental learning process. It involves two individuals who are seeking help and order a professionally trained person helping to First orient and diaries themselves towards a goal which leads to his maximum development and growth in his. And while there are immense levels of informal counseling, important counseling is done by elders for years without end training but is done better when some training is a human to a counselor now specialist counseling. It is the counseling which is done as part of the work of professional people such as nurse doctors professional counseling.

It is given by a fully trained professional person usually known as counselor. This training should consist of a masters or a B ha d in psychology or good yields and counseling with several years of supervised work. In the counseling nature of counseling the term counseling is often confused with a number of related terms which are in use in educational literature. Similarities between counseling and health education both aim at changing behaviors in order to reduce risk.

Both use two way interactions between provider and silent both really healthily communication skills counseling and motivation counselor is more effective than mediation as it is in its bide silence. While motivation means the healed personal in tears the coma session and the towards her highlights the advantage while a counselor talks of both avenues that this element is the moderator often makes a decision while counselor facilitates the silent to take a position. Counseling and otherwise the process is also different from the act of giving otherwise.

Counseling is a size to centerfield procedure dubbed by an expert varies various Wise is a non-technical person there which may be used by a teacher at pairings if friends are ever near at cancer in the time of need counseling anger deals. Counseling is a part of good deals, not all of it. It is special in the results part which deals with individual problems. Our counseling is good news but all good science is not counseling. Counseling counseling is used for normal persons who are troubled by some problem counseling is used in educational vocational and personal problematics stations.

It takes advantage of educational tests and techniques and handles the data together. Psychotherapy. It is used for sad sounds who have narrative problems. Psychotherapy is used in therapy parties. Our medical station makes use of various therapeutic techniques. It is such a suggested term to play in his country. I might add elements of counseling. It involves a person's counselor and count silly setting for counseling competence of counsel link counseling is assistance. Which the needy parsers cite.

General counseling. Established relationship between two individuals, one who is best served with problems etc. ceiling and the other who is professionally trained is at the giving and counsel demands free expiration of one's person proper down counseling increases the castle self-confidence. Counseling is a person's life process which depends on the dynamics of interpersonal relationships. Carson is the growth and development specific report communication and understanding change in feelings and expirations. Planning of counseling encourages you principle of counseling according to hand and McLean.

It is a staunch belief dedicated to south direction and self-regulation of the silent artist to then silence. Need is to be part first. It is preliminary. A preventive and mentally process work dictatorial attitude maintains a relationship of trust and confidence with the silent, letting the silence make voluntarily informed decisions. The sales family members in sang Higgins influencing personnel must be included in the counseling process to maintain the dignity of the individual as the individual is promoted to counseling.

Characteristics of counseling according to E. W. Feiler. It concentrates on the normal individual it considers breeds rather than that it involves a wide range of technical cues. It must be a co-operative affair and the counselor must egg as a point of contact. It shouldn't be solely based upon psychology skills required for effective counseling. Active listening reflecting for example silence. What do you think I should do about my wife's drinking problem? Nurse: What do you think you should do? Sam My sister wants help Abby told my mother's care.

I have to do it all, accusing them of a single idea or even a single world for example like you and I can discuss together offering General Lee's offer the silent encouragement to continue. For example, yes I see. Go on summarizing and for appraising for example silence. I can't stand it. My mind keeps wandering and knows you have difficulty concentrating. Silence. I can take that new job. What if I don't know you are afraid of you ? We fail in this new position and party observation realizing what is observed or perceived.

This includes the recognition of specific behaviors and comparing perception with the nerves. For example you think I'm twice you are pacing a lot. You seem uncle enforceable when you analyze each option with the silence the information given should include possible adverse reaction failures and ways to tackle them e.g. to adopt the family planning method by an eligible couple. The silence must be actively involved in the process of checking out the gains and costs involved in implementation of his hard position.

Non therapeutic communication techniques in counseling giving reassurance rejecting agree or disagree giving advice probing the founding using the Daniel approach for counseling. Director of counseling our consular center counseling steps of directive counseling synthetics diagnosis prognosis treatment or counseling follow up Annalise Evans thatch of directive counseling economical in time its emphasis the problem and not the individual the counselor can see the silence more objectively than the silence himself lays more emphasis upon intellectual rather than the emotional aspect of the personality of the individual.

The methods used are direct process you and explanatory limitation of counseling counseling doesn't gain any liability of self Emily's the car Sally is our depended on the counselor directive counseling doesn't guarantee that the counsel you will not make mistakes in future to non directive counseling assumption of non directive counseling. According to Carl Ray Ger man has dignity so he's stressed Wati the silent has the right to select off the goal of his life.

Steps of non directive counseling finding problematic station free expression of feeling positive and negative feelings classified development of inside termination of counseling station and vintage of non directive counseling. It is a slow but sure process to make the individual capable of making adjustments. Notice is used in eight and does one wise all debt is libraries and difficult. It removes the emotional block and helps the individual to reinterpret or is it out on conversation level terribly reducing the tension limitation on non direct counseling slow and time consuming process.

The counselor is expected to exercise excessive patience Eric Cary's high degree of motivation for the silent three eclectic counseling eclectic counseling defined as the sanctity and combination of direct two and non-threatening counseling. The counselor first takes into consideration the personality and needs of the counseling is sanction of eclectic counseling. It is possible to maintain a continuum from moderate to direct to metal steps of equity counseling making and tentative diagnosis analyses of the problem. Perhaps probation after a tentative plan for modifying factors securing effective conditions for counseling interviewing and stimulating the silence there will up his own resources limitation of eclectic counseling.

Elitism is not possible because direct you and nonthreatening concepts cannot merge together. Equity ism is reduced per visual and important estate tapes of counseling according to Harmer of prisons individual counseling group counseling tools and techniques used for individual counseling than their desired tools techniques intelligence chairman's aptitude interiors and personal to test non-standard EIS tools. Take kids question Mary interweave observation coming to record card case study rating scale CRM metric taken to group counseling.

It encourages themes of spirit and creates an acclimation of harmony, cooperation and understanding.

Is applied in homogeneous group passes of counseling. Phase Five termination and follow up phase four interaction Phase 3 setting goals Phase 2 assessment phase 1 establishing relationship good counselor always put the science needs first g good technical knowledge 0 updates a parole shared information from silent or object through we ask first questions they demonstrate proof and fuel now easy see confidential and maintained are observant.

Details - 1

You be saved and now I'm judgment is sensitive to needs of the silent e emphatic l listen effectively l led the silent made position of open mind. Ah respect the rise of the silence qualities of counselor interpersonal relationship personal adjustment vocational background held and personal Ypres leadership philosophy of life pers face your know dedication function of counselor program of good deals counseling and its organization orientation. Data collection Intel within individual counseling outside a Ganges placement and follow up problems in counseling grid system counseling either by counseling or by faculty calls you with different cultures.

The nursing students will come from different cultural backgrounds. They will have their own set of values and expectations. Counseling individuals is strong emotions such as anxiety and or depression intimacy which will hinder counseling process consular burnt out the symptom such as restlessness bred them irritability. Have fetch you negative feelings can the man is by changing girl environment approach taking care of themselves e.g. now sleep rest the eat play entertainment.

Others 3 Lack of awareness of all the valley of counseling by the public indicates administrators who set up a lack of physical facilities not aware Berti of assignment to start all training facilities for counselors' culture reasons for effective communication and counseling and effective communication skills used by a counselor. Failure to listen on the pulse of the counselor conflicting verbal and nonverbal messages a dash of mental attitude misunderstanding because of multiple meanings of English words false reassurance giving otherwise rather than encouraging the person to make decisions.

Applications of counseling nursing imply counseling helps improve in Bligh's mental health thus in changing understanding self control self-confidence and consequently their ability to work effectively improves upward and downward. Communication allows employees to express their feelings to management individual harms must be kept confidential e.g. directive to counseling a cure. When the counselor listens to employees' problems , they decide how to solve the problems and ask the employee what to do.

Outplacement counseling outplacement counseling can be used to minimize emotional informational scaring death results from being dismissed from one's position. Student counseling adjustment counseling crisis counseling marriage counseling vocational counseling behavioral counseling problem solving counseling dietary counseling motivational counseling physical logical counseling clinical counseling to keep moral Heike individual counseling Theory and Practice summary for effective counselor.

The most important instrument you have is your living example of who you are and how you struggle to live up to your potential. Be authentic. That's true deep professional roles can be shaped if you hide behind your role. The ceiling is also high to be a Terrapins UK person and be clear about who you are. Be willing to grow trees to care and to be involved.

Personal characteristics of effective counselors have an identity of respect and appreciate themselves, able to recognise and accept power open to change. Make choices which affect their lives, feel alive, make life oriented, choose alternative, sincere and—have a sense of humor.

Make mistakes and admit them, live in the present, embrace the influence of a sincere interest in the welfare of others involved in and drive meaningful Burke maintain healthy boundaries and ethical decision making. The principles that underlie our professional codes benefit others, do the harm, respect others autonomy, be jazz fair and faithful. The role of ethical courts they educate us about responsibilities are the basis for accountability protect clients are a basis for improving professional practice making ethical decisions identified a problem they were Eurobonds cards seek consultation brainstorm these consequences and decide silence rights sounds neat enough information about the counseling process to be able to make informed choice advocates silence about their rights and responsibilities.

Confidence showing is essential but not absolute. The silence poses a danger to other OS asylum under the age of 16 is the rate of abuse the silence needs to be hospitality if the information is made and used in a court action the. This creates a release of Ricard multiculturalism whose bases are reflected around we neglect social and community factors to focus on early on in the we do Elysium as it sounds with instruments have not been armed on the population they represent. Judges are physical. To college girl behaviors, beliefs or experiences that are normal far to silence killed her deal real to a sheep.

Some harmful questions we might have in a relationship keep me from confronting and challenging the silence.

Will my needs for relationships become more important than therapeutic activities? Can my silence manage to do a relationship as it is? My silence is my own. Can I talk, organize and professionally manage my attraction to my silent peace party? The development of personal t are all stage related to later mistrust and rejection issues as stage related delayed through personal poverty issues prowling stage related to leather safe soul and tattoos. To stage a time of socialization genitals stage sex saw and hour geez I am wasted in life.

The structure of personality the I.D. The demanding child rule abides appraisal principle, the angle the turkey calls ruled by the real principle. This super go. The judge ruled by the moral principle that in cars shoes clinical evidence for postulating the unconscious dreams slips of the tongue you piece hop naked segregation material derived from free suffocation material derived from projective technique cues symbolic content of physical tics symptoms note concepts nurses is only as to slice off the total mind involved defense mechanisms and or defense mechanisms are normal behaviors which operate on an unconscious level and tend to deny or disturb reality. The individual copes with anxiety and parents echo from behind.

Over loudmouths how adept you really are if they don't become a style of life to avoid facing reality this finality. Take because free association silence supports immediate Louise Howard Kent is suffering and feelings are towels interpretation trapeze points out explains and the meanings of what I wear is really the dream. Annalise therapies used the royal road to the unconscious to bring unconscious material to light transference and content transference transfers the silent Drakes to the therapist as he did to an earlier significant other.

The ALS the silent experience feelings that would otherwise be inaccessible and social transfers allows the silences you insight into the influence of the past contact transference third action after therapies thaws the silence that may interfere with objectivity resistance anything that votes against the process of therapy and parents the protection of Uncle shields material analyses of resistance had to silent to see that canceling appointments filing from therapy prematurely our ways of defending against anxiety these eggs interfere with the ability to accept change which could lead to a more satisfying life Lariam trophy Alfred Adler's individual psychology at phenomenological approach.

Social interest is stress at birth order and sibling relationship therapy as teaching you form again encouraging basing mistakes in the silence provides logic to deter a particular relationship. A collaborative partnership and the phenomenological approach at learning allows them to reach the wall from the silent subjective frame of reference of how life is in reality less important than how the individual believes life to be. It is not the childhood experiences that are curious so it is our present interpretation of these events and core skills in stakes and are passed down the term mine.

Our behavior, social interest and the small signification and distinctive concept refers to an individual's attitude toward an awareness of behind a part of the human common T. Mental health is measured by the degree to which we successfully share with others and are concerned with their wealth high happiness and sexes are largely related to social connectedness birth order and those five physical shekel positions. One oldest child receives more attention.

Paul Sandra of passion. Second of only two behaves as if Green era eyes often opposite the first child three men though after fears skews it out far younger as the baby face five only doesn't learn to share or co-operate with other children and learns to deal with dolls. Encouragement is the most powerful medal available for changing a person's beliefs helps build self-confidence and stimulate its coverage. This car demands the basic condition that lands people from functional need. Clients are encouraged to recognize that they have the power to choose and act differently.

Existential therapy is essential therapy physical Schickel intellectually approaches to therapy basic dimensions of the human condition and the capacity for self awareness. The tension between freedom and responsibility. The creation of an identity and establishing meaningful relationships. The search for meaning deception anxiety as a condition of leading the awareness of deed and non being the capacity for self awareness.

The greater our awareness the greater our possibilities for freedom. Veterans are realizing that we are finished T. Time is limited. We had the potential to act or not to act. Meaning is not ultimately we must seek it. We are subject to loneliness, meaninglessness , emptiness and is a nation identity and relationship. Identity is the courage to be. We must trust ourselves to search, retain and find our own answers.

Details - 2

Our great fear is that we will discover that there is no care or self relatedness at their best. Our relationships are based on our desire for fulfillment not our deprivation. Relationships that spring from our sense of deprivation are clinging parasitic and symbiotic. The Search for Meaning Meaning like Brazier meaning must be personal to all blue.

Clearly finding meaning in life is a byproduct of a commencement of creating loving and working. The real meaning is our BMI is thriving. Life is not meaningful in itself. The individual must create and discover meaning and exit a condition of living. Existential angst that is normal life cannot be lived nor can it be faced without anxiety. Exit the canvas devils for growth. As we become aware of and accept our freedom we can blind our exit by creating the illusion that there is sacred in life.

If we have the courage to face ourselves and life we may be frightened but we will be able to change the relationship between purpose and silence. Trap is a journey taken by trappers and silences the person to person relationship is gay. The relationship demands the therapist be in contact with their own phenomenological world. The car of the therapeutic relationship is respect and fade into silence. Potential to call sharing collection with genuine concern and in fighting person Sanford chirpy person centered trap a reaction against Drake Shu and psychoanalytic approaches challenge the assumption that the counselor knows best the wealthy to offer advice suggestion persecution teaching diagnosis and interpretation the belief that silence can not understand and resolve their own problems without dragged.

How to focus on problems over persons centered therapy emphasizes therapy is a journey shared by two fallible people. The person's innate striving for self causation, the personal characteristic of a therapist and the quality of a therapeutic relationship, the counselors creation of Burma's new growth promoting cool made people are capable of self directed role if involved in a therapeutic relationship. A girl promoting culture made Congress genuine loans are real and this unconditional positive regard sectors and caring but not approachable of all behavior equate empathetic understanding and ability to deeply Graves the silence subject to world Harper editors are more important than knowledge. 6 conditions 1 2 persons are in psychological contact 2 to.

The silence in experiencing incongruous see 3. The second person the therapist is conquered are greatest in the relationship for the therapist experiences unconditional positive Ranger are real caring for the silence 5 the therapist experiences in part far to silence internal frame of reference and and their years to culminate this the silence. 6 The communication to the silence is to a minimal degree achieved to disturb peace. Focus on the quality of the trip. What's your relationship? Serves as a model of the human being struggling toward greater illness is genuinely integrated and our ultimately without it falls.

France can openly express feelings and editors that are present in the relationship with this silence Gestalt therapy gift all to be existential and far more logical it is grounded in the silence here and now initial goal is for silence to gain awareness of what they are experiencing and doing now but almost died of experiencing rather than the abstractness of talking. Your boss's creations rather than talk about a hold true anymore does sound in Anchorage to become the heart child now.

Our power is in the present nothing ex's except now the past is gone and the future has not yet arrived. For many people the power of the present is lost. They may focus on their past mistakes and engage in endless relationships. Result is shun and silence for the future unfinished business. Feelings about the past express it. These feelings are associated with distinct memories and fantasies, feelings not full experience of languor and a background and interfere with Affective Contact result.

Pray call patient couples who behavior awareness or prayer Sue energy and self-defeating behavior liars of neuroses past Lang's are the unfolding of adults personality the peeling of an awning funny they are straws typical and in our antique forward layer fears keep us from seeing ourselves in past layer we give up our power Sue layer we fall experience our deadness explore sea layer we let go of funny rules contact and resistance to contact contact interacting with nature and with other people without losing once in the racially resistance to contact the defenses we develop to prevent us from experiencing the present Pu five my or channels of resistance interjection read throw faction deflection projection confidence tap what you technique used to experiment in gosh start happy preparing silence for experiments internal dialogue exercise rehearsal exercise revels so technically ex aggregation exercise reality therapy Yeah it's a basic beliefs and practices is our responsibility Tarif his function is to keep serving focus on the present.

We often mistakenly Charles misery in our best attempt to meet our needs we egg responsibility when we meet our needs without keeping orders from meeting their needs basic needs are internally matured behavior is jury it towers meeting one or more of our basic human needs longing power freedom found so while our brain functions as a control system forget us what to want crush does that lead the change the WD the E peace system W wants what do you want to be and do your picture album d do you the direction what are you doing. Why do you want to go?

E evolution that's your present behavior however is possible to get what you want P. Planning to change Senate is simple , easy to understand, specific and concrete, attainable routine campus days and duration of the silent measure able to change the observer label and how fully I embedded and involved what can be done today. Can you do C controls can you do this by ourselves or will you be dependent on others social behavior. Our best attempt to satisfy our needs is through behavior.

Thinking thoughts s statements feelings and your joy pain anxiety psychology Bob actions behavior terrified behavior therapy a set of clinical approach doors relying on experimental finding of psychological research based on principles of learning that our system of Collie bleed treatment goals are specific and measurable. Focusing on the silence current problems to how people change maladaptive thought that two behaviors to therapy is larger the occasional teaching silence skills of self management ex push your chair peace in rewards exam station but even graduate explorers sure to an actual figures station or Evan clothing prolonged and intense you in view are imaginable exposure to highly anxiety of walking similar without importantly to employ them a moment Zen station and yet processing and exposure based therapy that it was marginal floating combative.

Restructuring and the use of rhythmic eye movements and other bilateral stimulation to treat traumatic stress disorders and fearful memories of silence for expense of behavioral therapy one classical conditioning in classical conditioning Sartor's bond behavior such as the joys and celebration are elevated from a passive organism to a brand conditioning for cues on actions that operate on a very warm months to produce consequences if to every wrong mental change brought about by behavior is Ryan forcing the changes are strengthened at that the behavioral pure again if in realizing mental change produce no reinforcement.

That changed our lesson that the behavior real Sue for expected of behavior chirpy three soldier learning abroad should give us pro mice too there's Cipro so interactions between an individual's behavior and the and violent far commonly to be heavier Chappy emphasizes cognitive process and the wider ones as mediators of behavior change terror plots you take cues relaxation training to cope with threat I systematic DMCA shown for anxiety at the end it turns directions modern observational learning a action training social skills training self management program skewing psychology away multimodal trippy at technical expertise seem cognitive behavior chirpy racial emotive behavioral therapy stresses thinking. Judging, siding , analyzing and being assumes that cognitions, emotions and behaviors interact and how various sips should show cause and effect relationship.

Samples

The tactic is rarely direct to and concerned as much with thinking as with filling pages with our emotions. Mainly from our beliefs and relations interpretations and reactions to left station the church party process. Therapy is seen as an educational process. Clients learn to identify and dispute irrational beliefs that are maintained by self indoctrination.

30 plays in the park two ways of thinking would affect you and rational cognitions to stop absolutely speaking, thinking, blaming and repeating false beliefs. We are of human nature. We are born with the potential for bold rational and irrational thinking. We had a beautiful logical and killed world and Nancy to see us crawl carefully and to needlessly disturb ourselves. We learn and invent disturbing beliefs and keep ourselves disturbed by our self-talk.

We have the capacity to change our community IMO to and behavioral process rational ideas rational ideas lead to self-defeating behaviors. Some examples I must show are approachable from all the sacrifices and people in my life. I must perform this competently and perfectly if I don't get what I want is terrible and I can't stand it. Aryan bags. Cognitive therapy inside focus therapy emphasizes changing negative tools and money to leaves terrorist goals have shown people internal communication is accessible to interoperate sure silence believes have the personal meanings these meanings can be discarded by the silence rather than being told or interpreted by the term of these so are goals and principle of CDC basic salary.

To understand the nature of an emotional episode or disturbance it is irrational to focus on the cognitive concerns of individual reactions to this top upsetting. Our stream of thoughts. Does the change the way silencing by using the automatic tools the REACH THE CAR schmutz and begin to introduce the idea of shame restructuring principles automatic tools personalize three shows notations that are true Juliet's my part glory simile that lead the emotional response C D column it seems to her. Jean arbitrary inference. So I will throw away our generalization magnification and M.E. Zay showed personalization labeling and mis-leveling polarized thinking CTE cognitive treat pattern that triggers depression once silent halts negative we off down cells to sell it to abstraction.

Silent has a tendency to interpret experiences in another manner. 3 Silence has a gloomy vision and protection about the feature Donald, my Cambone cognitive behavior medication, proposed silence self globalization of self statements premise as a prerequisite to behavior change. Silence must not be how he felt and behaved. And what impact they have on others. Basic assumption that tracing emotions are typically used to resolve adaptive tools by hand bombs as B M self interaction will turn a you focus trained silenced or modified to insurrection.

They give to themselves so that they can cope emphasis is on curing practical coping skills cognitive structure the organizing spec of thinking which seems to monitor and dieted so choice of dollars the executor to process or which hauls the blueprints off thinking that this remind went to continue Interop or change thinking behavior change and copying three phases of behavior change one's self observation suits only in the internal deal. Three learning new skills coping skill programs stress inner escalation training.

While the conceptual phase skills a crucifixion and rehearsal phase 3 application and follow through phase construct to his narrative perspective for cues on stories people tell about themselves and others about signifies Evans in their lives to help his task have silence appreciate how they construct their realities and how they out or their own stories poems therapy key concepts of Hammond's surface problem are weaved in a socio political and cultural context the silence knows what is best for her life and is the experts on her own life emphasis is on advocating silence about the terror for fertile space traditional ways of sensing psychological health are challenges.

It is assumed that in the visual change will as a cure through social change science are encouraged to take social action for a push is to famines terror free one liberal feminism procures helping in the shall one overcome the luminous and constraining of their souls relation betters Mayor goals personal and programs of individual woman dignity self fulfillment a cult see to cultural feminism operations dreams from Sochi it is the relational forms threads emphasized the difference between woman and man believed the solution to oppression lies in feminization off to kilter soldier that becomes more nurturing cooperative and rational mayor.

The Goal of the trophy is the inclusion associated with Wales based on cooperation. Three radical feminism. Focus. The operation of a woman that is embedded in Petra. She seeks a change to associate its role. Activism terrifies Riyadh as a political enterprise with the goal of transformation of society. Major goals transform gender relationship transform Sollecito institutions increase one's sexual and procreative self-determination for socialist feminism also have goal sources told changed and on multiple operations believe salvation to associates problems must include consideration of class raise other forms of discrimination male goal of therapy is to transform social relationship and institutions.

Principle of feminist therapy is personal. The counseling relationship is agile or trim Waldman's experiences are Horner definition of distress and mental illness. I reform paid. There is an integrated analysis of Operation goals of fairness trophy the become aware of one's gender roles socialization process identify internalized gender role search and replace them with functional. Please take your skills to bring about change in the environment to do a wide range of behaviors that are freely chosen to become personal to improve over its integration technique is in feminist therapy gender role analyses and interaction to help silence understand the impact of gender role expectations in their lives.

Provide silence with insight into the way social issues affect their problems, power and others in power and domination and focus on the power difference between man and woman in society. How to recognize different kinds of power day passes and how they and others exercise power. Integration takes place in family therapy really or therapy allows the sands to make an informed choice. Reading a song means that address usually such as coping skills gender OF gender roles 30s way sexism is pro mod power differential between men and women socio it is obsession with genius self disclose sure to have it qualities to terror puts you relationship and provide modeling for asylum well is blue usable society and terror plot take iteration discuss assertiveness training woman become aware of their interpersonal rise tan skinned straight typical sex roles changed Nagato believes implement change in day of their lives reframing change the frame of reference for looking at an individual's behaviors shifting from an intra personal to an entire personal definition of a silence problem rebel link challenge label or a relation applet to the silence behavioral characteristics general.

The first cause is the shift from a negative to a positive revelation family systems therapy and the visuals are best understood through assessing the interactions we do and its family. Family symptoms are weaved as an impression offered this wine show within a family. Problematic behaviors so proposals for family are a function of the families an ability to operate pred actually are symptomatic batters handed down and Carol's generation of family isn't and directional you need and a change in one member affects all members as they are in family therapy and there is using educational model to counsel families and fences is on family atmosphere and family constellation trophies function as collaborators who seek to your join the family parent interweave sealed harms the about the pupils underlying children's misbehavior and later in families therapy goals luck mistaken goals in interaction all partners engage parents in the learning experience and then calibrate assessment phases is on the families motivational patterns main aim is to you need a great orientation after family multi generational family trophy the application of rational thinking to emotionally says rates system well at play tailor it is cost to be essential with the proper knowledge the individual can change.

Change occurs only with other family members differently shown after a psychological separation from others. Translation third party is Rick Reed's it's to raw dos excel the NSL is a couple's relationship multigenerational families have two goals. The change in New visual reads in the context of the system and generation to generation transmission of problems by solving emotional attachments less and X city and Andrew seem you believe symptom the increase in individual members level to differentiation human validation process model X handsome and a of self esteem family rules Congress and an openness in communication sculpting nurturing treats family mapping and chronologies human validation process model therapy Gulf open communication and the individuals are allow the half the report their perception enhancement of self esteem family physician are based on individual needs encouragement of growth.

Differences are an age and seen as a portion of his foreground transform extreme rules into useful and functional rules. Families have many spoken and unspoken rules experiential family therapy and free wheeling in only two sometimes out run Jules approach aiming to unmake his creative name meaning and liberate family members told themselves the keys are secondary to the terror particular relationship. Pragmatic end after school integration creates turmoil and intensifies what is going on here and now in the family experiential families have a glass still to get the wish.

In the vigil alternately and a sense of belonging in the family have individuals achieve more intimacy by increasing their awareness and they are experiencing. Encourage members to be down selves by freely expressing what they are thinking and feeling. Support spontaneity, creativity , the ABL to play and awareness to be crazy. Structural Family Therapy focuses on family interactions to understand the structure or urbanization after family. Symptoms are a byproduct of structural failings structural change miles to a cure. In a family before an individual's symptoms can bring ideas of dignity as are active, direct to and well sold out so their dual symptoms of these functions bring about structural change by modifying the family's transactional rules.

Developing more approaches shades boundaries. Creation of an effective hierarchical structure. It is assumed that faulty family structures weigh boundaries that are rigid or diffuse subsystems that have in approach Shri task and functions strategic family therapy focus on solving problems in the present presenting problems are accepted as real and not a symptom and system these function therapies are brief process focus and solution oriented.

The turf is the sighing strategies for change that result when the family falls off the therapies direction and change transaction thrusts strategic family turf goals are still present problems. By focusing on behavior real sicknesses get people to behave differently. Shift a family organizations sorted presenting problem is no longer functional multifamily Tolbert appreciates stage or family they will augment problems often arise during interim station from one developmental stage to annex social constructionism the silent not the therapies is expert deal which is used for Ellis's bar spectral resources and unique sales experiences questions and were family members to speak and express their desert positions the tariff is sublease optimism and to process social costs react to these events horrific goals generate new meaning in the lives of family members Kogelo feeds families solid shells that are unique to the station exchange awareness of the impact of varies as back often dominant kilter on the family how families develop alternative ways of being acting now living and leaving.

At Lake structural very therapy and therapy to resume how many therapists does it relate to change in life allow just one but the light bulb has to want to be change racial while for ESPN SBT brief model of the terrorism look the way it sounds to overcome their resistance silence stay in treatment for from six to ten incisions Silence report maximum gains after three to six Asians but terror for models have you found to have no SAT and fund some difference in their effects owners than those of long term terror for models therapies who halt to a brief terror from model how well is and believe about what can and cannot be accomplished in therapy bleep effective therapy result in the early resolution of Karen's problems and not end of May or modification of personality of character structure below.

Their job is to face leaks rather than build a custom designed house from the ground up. Excellent behavior which reflects confidence in the efficacy of the established challenging but limited goals for treatment work solvers inside but also facilitates behavior change.

Results

Their primary goal is to initiate a healing process that can continue through all halt to the silence leaves. Why people seek out brief therapy. Most people don't decide. Lampley process and cower of substitutions and conversations arise. They are vague about their mental health. They say our therapy because they are in the same form of currencies which affects their mental well-being.

They want to find coping strategies which will assist them to elevate their current experience of pain. Be of therapy helps silence identify whether or not they are blind. Bob's awaiting to be changed see Eve and match axis in their temperament and personality styles. With herpes. See if the right mix of moderation and simpatico between silence of therapies such change then a cure. In a brief period of time if there is not a match therapies need to encourage them to not be used as therapy until every readiness and willingness to do what dates to change so that they can turn on light bulbs.

Literature on brief therapy leaders' improved therapy includes Bennett Badman Cummings who shares her Harley the M R I grew up on fake land fish SIEGEL And what's Loic strap and been there. Tell them and Wells reviews after his search who bizarrely have found brief therapy as effective as time Alimi. The traditional trope is regarded as a diagnosis all duration of treatment long term trophies one seek change in the basic character to believe that second of kind psychological change is unlikely. In everyday life three see you presenting problems as reflecting more basic pathology.

I want to be there as silence makes magnificent change, five seats happy as having a timeless quality and works if sounds are willing to wait for change. Six and consciously recognize physical conventions of man thing long term Saddam's seven leave psychotherapy as almost always been good and useful 8 C sounds be in he as the most important part of silenced life short term therapies. While prayer for pragmatism parsimony and Lee's radical interrogation and don't believe in the notion of cure to maintain is our development perspective from Reed's significant psychological changes removed as you know with Table 3 emphasized sounds strange and research presenting problems are taken seriously.

For said many change will occur after church chirpy and will not be observe label to the Territory's 5 don't accept timeless of some models of therapy six fiscal years of two moods either by the nature of the therapies for practice or structure for Ryan rhyme burst among seven we've psychotherapy as being sometimes useful and sometimes harmful. 8 So being in the world is more important than being in therapy. Assumption about silence. In brief therapy models the silence of her experience of faulty learning at some point in early life.

The silence and their her environment intrigue and infidels each other reciprocally. The interpersonal environment of the silence in their natural environment influences the sounds positively or negatively although personality character Sadr's supporters are all very important in people's life, better change in currents and change. Allen's are also prominent factors in shaping lives cause people understand experience at least in part on the basis of their stage of development. There will be little to no turpitude until the silence are read of the change critical surface factors in brief therapy Tempest Moss maintain clear specific perk schools and structure maintain acts you to a particular role by suggesting activities are either sides collaborating as problem solving using case homework assignments by asking questions remain aware of the real and of time in says each season.

B as well as retail too does the size outcomes make time with resolution spending clarity on the turpitude process by homework assignments readings journal writing break ties of new behaviors such as exercise joint self Hap robes public speaking and volunteering and trying new interaction all patterns in the family marriage and work or school setting. If applicable critical therapies factors so embrace therapy therapist MOS try new strategies something different. Novels to motivate and challenge science to deal with the presenting problem successfully are flexible.

Equity in ready of treatment modalities for individual couple family group use in the words you seasoned racial and should duly see end of treatment as interrupting terminating encourage silence recognize therapy is a process all worthwhile life cycle and can return on an as needed basis because with the silence lapse is a part of recovery to return to terror p is not failing but good common sense. Recognize these incentives because training programs to manage therapies finances survival need the silence factor in brief therapy. Come to believe that just five people a night a person of all silence are appreciated for belief therapy.

Cough and shine indicate that individuals who appear to benefit miles from breathe therapy are health problems that had a sudden and acute onset. Very probationers, their G zone label will adjust the world will stay well with others head high initial motivation in turning the therapeutic process moved to if you may be in appreciation. For individuals wills personal characteristics are in contrast to those not at all and some types of psychological disturbances substance abuse psychosis and personality disorders silence fades and brood therapy to silence mass.

How our age, intellectual ability and ability to understand do issues involve being able to read and write in order for many of the excitements to be psychologically minded and open to psychological answers inside interpretation and suggestion of some social support system in place where they can turn for support and understanding during dead time in the therapeutic process. We must be motivated to change light bulbs that already have social orientation and pose problems in the social context that have clear prison problems. Our principal complaint which can be identified in therapy is the ability to call a way to return. In the process science factors in brief therapy 2D science must have been able to have established at least one meaningful relationship in their lives.

How couples dysphoria but emotional involvement and a clear rapid emotional separation. However strained have the ability to express feelings and have the expectation that therapy will successfully be excluded based on the belief that therapies don't try to treat the untreatable trespass thing. All therapy trial therapy for three seasons and either transfer in appropriate silence use after two or and Jack team models of treatment are often no tradesman characteristic of aggregate extraction library therapy one third tackle this is to lanes of seizure three free clients and regular ads of season's far duration of treatment five location of therapy cease initiation of therapy so termination of therapy et girls old Toby nine therapeutic process ESB to model flexible process of tricycle integration one limits of any color it is set realistic goals similar to reality Toby collaborative relationship between therapies and silence similar to person centered Toby rapid and early assessment done by Jobe is of lies and technique is from systemic family therapy purpose interrogations similar to the multimodal behavioral therapy staying centered in the here and now we decide loans similar to existence these the therapy ESB team model flexible process of 30 article integration to direct activity accomplished by the silence similar to cognitive therapy ventilation of emotions similar to the guest of therapy teaching how to identify and review the irrational thinking similar to rational emotive behavior.

Taylor finds challenging and confronting psychological defenses similar to psychodynamic therapy encouraging personal responsibility, intercepting the social consequence for one's actions similar to add real therapy creative and Ephesians use of time selection process by which suitable sellers who are light bulbs read need to be turned on and rolled. Is these thread month model goal of technical D in e SBT strengthen

Redmond's gaze Gen analyze learning from season to real expertise love for learning of knife skills are in changing of and altered to power silence who are or reside that and feel like outcast neighbors silence the person Zeit therapy as something which they have done on their own we've selves as competent self healers who can gain the coping skills and exchange.

Old ones enabled through Eve self confidence increases self words and a sense self esteem tapes of take these in e SBT aging aimed at exploring styles presenting problems gain understanding challenging and at assisting sounds to challenge their dolls emotions and actions can clear these and add a blazing silence process and degree of change in two teams take rookies of ESB to conduct a procession telephone call mail are psychosocial medical historian forums assertion in the initial season if salads are ready for treatment or if someone else is pressuring them into treatment exiles how soon they expect to be helped and what they see to be the OPs tacklers train salads in problem analyst and goal setting explain the land and to nature of ESB tradesmen keep silent in the here and now operate in assumption length of trade means only one season Meyer initiating message in SBT or parents did the best they called knowing what they did at time we as adults must now take responsibility for our own lives and learn what normal is so that we can hail healthier more productive lives.

Challenging task because in the SBT Homer had the silent invasion change used novel to uncommon therapy used rundown position column bull use humor in threat work to silence robust and kill family utilize metaphor or paradox use crystal ball technique cue as challenging questions of silence and call to be blitz therapy Holmberg in ESB te self esteem development lifestyle of record a family of origin behavior interjected streets and ERO facial believes the gloss personal growls and in relationship communications and or work out handling control issues.

Healing the inner child for self healing tears system thoughts emotion action Elo system essays listen is out relax take steps Andrew system said namely to get it out exercise release let go system lighten need exercise right take steps you up control order life charts use them calm heal inform lighten dregs love system recognize exercise low ect Protech support ever live trade c system. Mind Body Connection brain racial reasoning head god in loser of any system heart rate praise or gastric acid.

Abalone lonely immune system conquered using keys pulse rate and sculpting Journal Review sizes conduct therapy season with self contract silence to try its own no therapy imagery were silent is it their time you silently a process perk how these tips consistently fail in brief therapy don't attempt so presenting problem of the sales dealing with the silence past is essential.

Deal with it extensively focus only on symptoms Braddock a worsening of the symptoms are symptoms substation our focus on silence their noses and streets area necessary for diagnosis you must use on the one terror article framework Don't be to assume change must be observe label to be real change insist all years of treatment to bring about challenge our girl in the sounds ignored the silence waiting quick results don't define goals in therapy don't collaborate with your silence assume our responsibility for success or failure the silence in therapy don't average late your effectiveness.

Don't miss out!

Visit the website below and you can sign up to receive emails whenever Gaurav Sanjiv Kalangan publishes a new book. There's no charge and no obligation.

https://books2read.com/r/B-A-EPFBB-UHIRC

BOOKS2READ

Connecting independent readers to independent writers.

Also by Gaurav Sanjiv Kalangan

Learn Options Strategies Options Basics & Greeks For Stock Trading By Technical Analysis
Bitcoin, Altcoins & ICOs Learn the Basics of Digital Coins from Zero
Time Management This Is How I Work 300 Percent Faster